Praise for *Living in Interesting Times*

"This is a book for which many of us have been waiting, whether we knew it or not. We joke that "May you live in interesting times!" is a curse, and many of us have been feeling a bit as though that applies to our lives. The important question is "What can we do about it?", because there is more to do than just hand-wringing!

Catherine Kane has pulled together a list of very practical ways of coping when life gets hairy, and, thank goodness, it's also short enough for even the most harried to get through. She starts with explaining how the physical and energetic world interact, and goes on to provide clear instructions on building up good energy, getting rid of and shielding yourself from negative energy, and dealing with the energies that you didn't create or invite in, but have to deal with anyway. Although talking about energy, the suggestions she provides are concrete and practical. Sure, it would be easier if we didn't have to deal with problems, but was there ever a time people didn't? And since we have to live with it, it's wonderful to have a handy guidebook for negotiating life in this time."

-Tchipakkan
Metaphysical speaker teacher and artist,
Host of The New Normal" on www.liveparanormal.com,
Co-founder of Changing Times, Changing Worlds metaphysical conference

"I wish I had this book "Living in Interesting Times" when I was first becoming aware of my own abilities. Her style is informative but the information is given in a fun playful way, which makes the reader feel like you're having a conversation with Cathy. It's an easy read and a very enjoyable one too."

-Reverend Freya Harris-Scarpa
Licensed interfaith minister, healer and teacher

"A perfect guide to dealing with energy for beginners or the more experienced trying to navigate the issues that arise in the world today. Full of tips on how to be aware of where our energy is going and what's pulling us down - and how to fix that - that anyone can use. The author has gift for writing in a way that is both engaging and easy to access for any reader. I look forward to adding this to my library."

- Morgan Daimler,
author of Fairycraft and Fairies

And also for Catherine's previous books

Magick For Pennies

"Magick For Pennies is a wonderfully down to earth metaphysical guidebook full of both the basic how-to of magical practice and practical tips for the frugal practitioner. A great combination of common sense advice, encouragement to trust your own intuition, and creative ways to make the most of what you've got. Beginners and experienced folk alike will find something useful in this book."

Morgan Daimler,
author of Fairy Witchcraft, Pagan Portals: The Morrigan, and By Land, Sea, and Sky

Manifesting Something Better

"The techniques in this book are invaluable. Who said wishes are for children? Catherine shows you how to use positive energy in a way that is simple, direct, as well as very effective. I have used many of these techniques myself with nothing short of wonderful results. So make a wish, simply ask for it. Wouldn't it be wonderful if everyone read this book and learned how to make their life happier, healthier, and just that much more Wonderful?"
-Alexis Doyle
 Internet radio show host

The Practical Empath-
Surviving and Thriving as a Psychic Empath

"…Gives you a window of understanding as to who an empath is, a brief synopsis about energy and how it works, shielding techniques, how much input is too much, and so much more. Cathy is an amazing empath who has helped countless people to learn how to deal with this wonderful however sometimes daunting gift. This book makes a great read for the novice and the experienced empath alike. With Cathy's guidance, you will learn how to cope with being an empath and, hopefully, you will get as much, if not more, out of her book *The Practical Empath* as I did. Happy reading."
-Delilah Kieffer, spiritualist and psychic

Adventures in Palmistry

"The information in this book is clear, concise, hits the pertinent points of palmistry, and immediately lets you start practicing your craft."
-Adam Latin, professional palmist

"Ms. Kane is not only a talented palm reader, but a talented writer as well. She explains the concepts and techniques clearly, and with a sense of humor."
-Lois Fitzpatrick, leader, East Kingdom Soothsayer's guild, which studies the methods and history of psychic readings

The Psychic Power of Your Dreams

Once again Catherine Kane has created a wonderfully accessible experience, like a visit with your fairy godmother with cocoa and cookies, wrapped up in an easy to read book. Have you been wondering if your dreams have something important to tell you? and if they do, how do you figure it out?

People have been writing dream interpretation books since the time of the Pharaohs, in Greece, Rome, and the Middle Ages, ..right up to the present, because humans spend a third of their lives dreaming, and the centuries have proven the value of paying attention to dreams. What makes this book especially valuable is that she recognizes that all dreams are not the same and cannot be read the same way. She describes many sorts of dreams and how you can work with them. (If your nightmare is from indigestion, better lay off the spicy snacks before bed!) How to tell the difference between literal and symbolic psychic dreams, and how to decipher your own personal symbol set (because your dreams don't use someone elses'). So this is not a book where you can look up crocodile, and read "If a man sees himself in a dream eating crocodile flesh it is good omen, meaning he will become a village official." (Yes, that's one of the Egyptian ones.)

Going beyond that, Cathy gives you lots of helpful hints (as any good fairy godmother would), about how to remember your dreams better, how to program your dreams, how to get the messages your dreams are trying to send; in short, she has a bit of something for everyone, delivered in a relaxed, friendly manner, that will make exploring these new skills easy and fun.

-Tchipakkan
  Co-chair Changing Times- Changing Worlds conference
  Metaphysical speaker, teacher and artist

The Lands That Lie Between

This book is an urban fantasy, the story of a girl who leaves home with her cat, moves across country, and starts a new life. After getting a tarot reading her fresh start gets a twist though when magical things start to happen around her. At first Morgan dismisses the strange events, but soon she finds herself embroiled in an adventure - with her trusty cat by her side - to find a gateway into Fairy and help choose the new king before the bad guys get to her and take her out. Fast paced and fun, with like-able characters and touches of genuine mythology interwoven with the authors story, it's reminiscent of old fairy tales or quests. The book has a light tone, and although it does include some violence and adult themes it would be appropriate for younger readers, or for older readers looking for something light and enjoyable. I'm looking forward to more from this author and hope this turns into a series.
-Morgan Daimler,
  author of Fairy Witchcraft, Pagan Portals: The Morrigan, and By Land, Sea, and Sky

Living in Interesting Times:

Practical Energy Work When Times Get Tough

By Catherine Kane

Also by Catherine Kane

Adventures in Palmistry

The Practical Empath-
Surviving and Thriving as a Psychic Empath

The Lands That Lie Between-
An Urban Fantasy with Morgan and Sam

Manifesting Something Better-
Easy, Quick and Fun Ways
To Manifest the Life Of Your Dreams

The Psychic Power of Your Dreams:
Practical Skills for Working With Your Dreams For Insight, Information, Creativity and a Better Life

Magick for Pennies:
Affordable Metaphysics for Everyone

For more information, please visit Foresight Publications at www.ForesightYourPsychic.com

Living In Interesting Times:
Practical Energy Work When Times Get Tough

By Catherine Kane

Living In Interesting Times: Practical Energy Work When Times Get Tough©October2017
by Catherine Kane

All rights reserved.

No other part of this book may be reproduced or transmitted in any form, or by any means, electronic or mechanical, including photocopying, recording or by any information storage and retrieval system, without written permission from the author, except for brief quotations in a review.

ISBN 978-09846951-4-0

**Foresight Publications
Wallingford, CT.**

Dedications

This book is dedicated to my family, who've taught me a lot about positive energy, looking for solutions and hanging in there no matter what happens;

And also to my beloved Starwolf, who's got my back in interesting times, both great and small.

With all my love,

Catherine

Acknowledgements

Here we are, in the fall of 2017, and we are certainly living in interesting times indeed. As always, while my name is on the cover, there's a lot of other special people who have made this book possible and I'd like to say some thank-yous here.

To the readers/ reviewers who told me what worked in this book and what needed work, thanks. Kudos upon kudos to Jayee White Oak, Morgan Daimler, Tchipakkan and Rev. Freya Harris, who help me make these books more useful, helpful and fun.

Special thanks to Tchipakkan and Starwolf, for research, specialized information and brainstorming above and beyond the call of duty.

To the leaders and members of the Fairfield County Writer's Group- a writer needs a tribe, and you're one of the best I could imagine.

To my readers, both old friends and new ones. Welcome. Here's wishing that your times are only as interesting as you want or need them to be, and that this book helps you when such times come.

And one more acknowledgement for my husband Starwolf. He's been with me from the beginning of this writing journey and his love and support are part of the reason I can do what I do. Love you, dear

Table of Contents

Introduction 1
1- About This Book 3
2- How Energy Works 5

Let's Start at the Heart 9

3- Do You Need to Protect Your Energy? 11
4- Shielding to Protect Your Energy 15

Clearing Negative Energy 23

5- Grounding Unwanted Energy 25
6- Clearing Your Mind 35
7- Mind the Gap 43

Being More Aware 49

8- Noticing What's Happening 51
9- Know What Drains You 57
10- Stop the Drain 63

Building Your Positive Energy 71

11- Know What Strengthens You 73
12- Make Nurturing Yourself a Priority 79
13- Build More Positive Energy 85

The Energy Around You 95

14- Warding to Protect Your Space 97
15- Crystals and Energy 105

16- Your Space and Positive Energy 111
17- Find Your Tribe 117
18- Taking Control 125

Positive Energy For Life 131

19- Check Where You're At 133
20- Rinse, Repeat, Build a Routine 137

Living in Interesting Times 147

Appendix 149

A Light in The Forest 151
The Book of Answers 153
Time Travel 155

Glossary 157
Index 161

Introduction

There's an old joke about a curse that goes "May you live in interesting times…" It's a joke, but, like most good jokes, it's funny because it holds a kernel of truth inside of it.

All of us, at one point or another, have lived in "interesting times". We've been through times of fear and struggle and overwhelming odds. We've walked through the shadows, with no clue of what lay ahead and whether we would come out of the darkness and into the light again.

That can be hard on a person. It's stressful and draining and can test you far beyond what you thought were your limits. It can strain your health. It can damage your emotional and psychological wellbeing. It can reset your energy into negative levels. It can leave you with permanent scarring, whether you make it through the darkness or not.

And that's what this book is about. It's about ways to pass through the darkness with your light still shining. It's about ways to keep your energy positive. It's about ways to control how much negative energy you take in, how much negative energy you hold onto, and how to avoid damage or heal it if you can't avoid it. It's about practical methods, both energetic and mundane, to make it through the darkness and come out on the other side with your soul whole.

I'm sitting here in the middle of the night in a darkened house, typing away in interesting times. It's less than a week after the inauguration, and there's a lot of fear and anger and bigotry and revolution out there.

And we're all going to be alright. We will come through these interesting times.

I'm writing this book to help with that, but I think

it's important to note that this book can also help in other "interesting times". Health crises. Family emergencies. Financial challenges.

The same techniques that can help you keep your center during societal changes can also help during personal ones. Just find the ones that work for you, and remember to use them when times get tough

Keep your head; keep your center; and come through those interesting times…

Chapter One
About This Book

Let's take a moment to talk about how this book works. In most of my other books, I have an initial section that covers groundwork on the topic we're discussing, followed by a more open section of different approaches you can use to deal with it. I think of it as a kind of informational "all you can eat buffet," where you can take the pasta salad, skip the casserole and load up on the sliced beef, according to your own tastes and preferences.

This book is a little different. It's built as a series of steps.

- First, we look at how energy works and how it can affect the quality of our lives.
- Then we look at protecting and clearing our own personal energy.
- We look at being aware of our energies and what's happening with them.
- We examine what feeds our energy and what drains it.
- We look at protecting the energy of our space and having our environment support positive energy.
- And last, we develop a long term plan to make this work for us in all the times of our lives.

Now, you have free will and can work with this information as you like. Because this is a series of steps, though, I think you'll probably get the most good out of it if you do it in order.

I find people tend to fall into two learning types- the ones who like to work a process step by step and the ones who like to go all the way through first to get the big picture and then go back and work through it. Either way's good, but it's a good idea to work the steps sequentially, so you get the most out of this.

That being said, welcome to Living in Interesting Times, a book about practical energetic techniques for dealing with the times that challenge us.

Hoping you find things here that fit your needs and make your life better.

Chapter Two
How Energy Works

Let's look at energy and how it works in our lives.

We all have individual energy fields that surround us. Our fields all vibrate at different rates. The higher your vibrational rate, the better you'll feel. The lower your rate of vibration the more down or depressed or negative you'll be. This works in both directions; if your vibration's higher, you'll feel better and if you choose a positive attitude, you'll boost your vibration higher.

Your rate of energetic vibration is affected by a number of things like

- Your health.
- Your beliefs.
- Your experiences.
- Your attitude.
- What's going on in your life right now.
- What you give your attention to.

It's not just set by your beliefs about the world and what's happening. Other people's energetic fields can affect yours. (You can be "slimed" by other peoples' energy…)

We all have a default level of vibration we tend to fall back into when we're not making conscious choices and when the world isn't affecting us. If you tend to be a positive thinker, your vibration tends to stay more in the higher levels. If you focus mostly on what's wrong with the world, your energy tends towards a lower vibration

That's important to know, because a higher vibrational level feels good, a lower one feels lousy, and it's helpful to know the habits that take you in directions you'll enjoy (or that you won't.)

And there's other reasons to want a higher energetic level besides that it feels good…

Positive thinking and higher vibrations tend to have a positive effect on your health. Folks with positive vibrations tend to:

- Be healthier,
- Have less accidents,
- Avoid catching illnesses,
- Heal quicker,
- Need less medication,
- Have a more resilient mindset that lets them adapt better to circumstances, whatever they are.

Negative people tend to get sick or hurt more and have more problems coping or recovering.

It's a powerful argument for positive thinking…

In addition to feeling better and being healthier, there's another good reason to try to keep your energy higher and more positive. It's called the Law of Attraction.

The Law of Attraction is one of a set of rules that define how energy works. In its simplest form, the Law of Attraction says that Like attracts Like. This means that when your energetic vibration is at a certain level, it tends to attract other people, things and experiences that also vibrate at that level.

How does your energy get to that level? What you focus on most tends to set that vibration. So, if you spend most of your time focusing on chocolate chip cookies, you'll attract more chocolate chip cookies; and, if you spend most of your time concentrating on all of the bills you have to pay, you'll attract more bills.

You don't just attract more of the same though. You'll also attract more people, things and experiences that are not the same thing, but that vibrate at a similar level. So, if you give your focus to chocolate chip cookies, you'll not only attract more chocolate chip cookies, but also more hot fudge sundaes.

In general, that means that the higher your vibration is, the more likely you are to attract more of the kind of things you want, and the more your vibration drops, the more likely you are to attract things you don't want.

That's a good incentive for boosting your vibration higher and keeping it there. We'll be talking about how to do that later in this book.

You have free will and the right to choose how you live your life, but while you're making those choices, it's good to know the things that'll help you have a better life and the ones that get in the way of it.

A higher vibration feels better, supports your health and better choices, and attracts more of the things that you want into your life while giving you more protection from being affected by negative energy around you. Positive energy is worth considering, and this book is here to show you ways that you can raise your energy up and keep it up.

There's lots more on energy in the chapters coming up…

Let's Start at the Heart

Chapter Three
Do You Need to Protect Your Energy?

In the last chapter, we talked about energy and how it works. The next question is whether we need to protect our energy fields, and, if we do, how much? In energetic circles, there are lots of different opinions about metaphysical protection…

- Do you need metaphysical protection?
- If so, when do you need it?
- How much?
- What kind?
- How do you protect yourself and those you care for?

Opinions vary widely. Some people believe that "the Universe is a friendly place" and that, as long as you keep your thoughts and energy positive, you'll never draw anything negative to you. These folks tend towards minimal protection, believing positive focus manifests a
positive world around them.

Some people believe that the magickal world is a war-zone, full of negative energies and entities that'll as soon do you harm as look at you. These folks tend to ward, pray, or invoke at every contact with the non-physical world, regardless of degree.

I tend to fall in the middle. I see the magickal world as having good neighborhoods and bad ones, kind of like the material world. Like the material world, the degree of protection needed varies with the neighborhoods I visit and the activities I engage in there.

For instance:

- In a church with an emotionally healthy congregation- not so much protection is needed.

- In a house where someone has died violently, I may need more protective activity.
- When I'm showing someone how to use acupressure to ease a sinus headache- minimal protection needed.
- When I'm reading for someone in the process of resolving PSTD (post-traumatic stress disorder) – more protection needed.

You may not only need protection against hostile beings or energetic attacks. Psychic protection can also help you avoid being overwhelmed by the energy of people in crisis or places that are off-kilter. In such cases, people may not intend to harm you, but you can be battered or thrown off balance by the experience anyway. Protective practices can be like wearing a metaphysical hard-hat; helping to keep your head straight and safe so you can deal with what's happening.

So how much psychic protection do you need?

To a certain extent, your beliefs can shape the world around you. This means that what kind and how much protection you need, as well as when you need it, is based in part on your circumstances and in part on your beliefs about those circumstances. I'd encourage you to learn to listen to your inner wisdom and to trust it on when you need psychic protection (or, for that matter, regular protection) and how much you need.

- Don't feel right about that guy in the garage? Have someone walk you to your car.
- Feel prickly and nervous with no obvious cause? A prayer might be in order.
- Feel safe using a pendulum to answer questions at a friend's place? You probably don't need further protection there.
- Feel uneasy about reading for someone? You might want to increase your energy shields, pray or contact

your guardian spirits; or you might not want to read at all. This might be the wrong time, the wrong place or the wrong person to read for.

In future chapters, you'll see lots of ways to protect your energy. Use what speaks to you when you feel like you need it. Don't feel you need to use every technique but don't try and "tough it out" if you feel like you need protection. Don't assume that your needs will be the same as the person next to you- it's not a one size fits all universe, and we've got to do what works for us as opposed to someone else.

What you need is what you need- no more and no less. Listen to your inner wisdom. It was put there for a reason.

14

Chapter Four
Shielding to Protect Your Energy

In the last chapter, we looked at metaphysical protection. Do we need it? How much do we need? What kind? Now let's take a look at some basic ways of protecting our own energy.

When looking at energetic protection, we need to start with our own energetic fields. We're all surrounded by a series of layers of personal energy, collectively known as an aura. When negative things or energy come into our auras, they can cause negative experiences for us, such as illness, accidents, fear, energetic drain or other things that most people would rather not experience. As they pass through the layers of our auras, their effects get stronger the closer they come to our physical bodies.

Furthermore, if you're repeatedly exposed to negative energies over the long term, they can "take up residence" in your aura, and have a cumulative effect. Did your mother ever say "If you hold that face long enough, it'll stick that way?" Mine did. Negative energy can act that way:

- If you hang out with people who are habitually cruel;
- If you live in a place with chronically toxic energy and don't clear that energy;
- If you're an empath surrounded by drama queens;
- And so forth....

you can develop a case of chronic negative energy and chronic problems to go with it.

If you're caught in a pattern of chronic exposure to negative energy, the techniques and other remedies (such as crystals) in this book can come in handy; but you'll still need good energetic shields.

Whether you're dealing with empathic overload,

psychic vampires, metaphysical attack or a toxic environment, one of your primary defenses is good energetic shields. Good shields surround your energetic field, keeping out things that could harm you. Picture them as being kind of like a science fiction-type force field.

Let's walk through how to develop energetic shields.

Good energetic shields are a good idea. They protect you from negative or unwanted energy. They let you keep your energy separate from the energy of others. They make it easier for you to control your own vibrations. They help you keep your head clear so that you can make better decisions

But how do you get good energetic shields? You can't just go to the local department store and pick them up in the "energetic shields" department.

Here's a basic exercise for developing your own energetic shields.

Whenever you have a moment (or two or ten…) close your eyes and picture yourself surrounded by light. Light on the left of you and the right; light in front of you and in back; light over your head and under your feet; so that you're surrounded completely on all sides by light.

What color should the light be? Tradition holds that it should be white, as that is the highest/ purest/ best color and also contains all other colors within it. I say you should chose whatever color makes you feel safest/ calmest/ best with yourself.

- Like green? Great!
- Want Pink? Right on!
- If you want plaid, I'm for it!

You can also have more than one color. My own shields tend to be white with a gold edge.

As you visualize this light, set an intention to define what your shields will do for you. What's setting an intention? Just a fancy new age term for setting a goal for what you're doing energetically and holding it in your mind while you work. In the case of shields, setting an intention could be:

- Intending that you will be protected from any energy that could harm you in body, mind or spirit;
- Intending that no energy will directly touch you unless you consciously chose to let it;
- Intending that you will be aware of the energy surrounding you, but that it cannot affect you;
- Intending that your shields are always protecting you unless you consciously chose to let them down.

You get the idea. What would you like your shields to do?

As you work on your shields, you'll find over time that you feel more protected and more able to cope with energy that surrounds you. Once your basic shields are functioning, you can tweak your visualizations and/or your intent to fine-tune your shields to best meet your unique needs.

That's the basics on how to start developing your energetic shields.

After you've been working on building up your basic energetic shields for a while, you'll probably find that you're getting better control over how the energy around you affects you. You'll have more ability to choose- chose what energy you let in and what to keep outside of you.

But what if your shields aren't always strong enough?

In every life, there are challenging times, times that particularly test us- even if we have great shields.

- In the face of bigotry;
- In the malls at Christmastime;
- When the one you love is really, **really** ticked at you.

We all face times when the stakes are high, the energy is flowing double-time (…or triple-time, or a hundred-fold…), and our shields feel like we've built them out of swiss cheese (nice, but full of holes).
What to do?
This is the point at which you give your shields an upgrade. Start with the basic shields. Set your intention (remember how?) that the basic shields you're building are on at all times, unless you consciously chose to take them down. Add a further intention that, at times that are energetically challenging, you can consciously or unconsciously choose to improve those shields to meet your personal needs.
What do I mean by "improve"? Well, you can make your shields:

- Stronger;
- Thicker;
- More resilient (so negative energy bounces off and far away);
- More powerful;
- More energetic (up the amps);
- More adhesive (so negative energy gets stuck at the edge and can't reach you);
- Any combination of the above;
- Or any other concept that works for you.

In tough times, I like to mentally "flare" the energy in my shields and then push the extra energy outwards with my mind. It makes my shields feel stronger and more powerful, and gives me more control on what outside energy

I accept.

Once you've got the basic shields in place, it's good to add an improved upgrade to your routine, and get it in place as a familiar practice while times are relatively calm. This means that, when you have a need for it, you'll have built both the upgraded shields and the habit of using them.

And you'll be ready for whatever Life brings you…

We've talked about basic and improved energetic shields. Now let's look at tweaking energetic shields to serve the specific needs of an empath.

What's an empath? A psychic empath (as opposed to someone who's psychologically empathetic, something totally different) is a particular type of psychic who's really tuned in to feelings and emotional vibrations. Empaths receive information from these "vibes" which can be useful for things like truly connecting with and understanding people, resolving difficulties, motivating folks and knowing who to trust (amongst other things.)

Many people are psychically empathic, which makes them more vulnerable to the emotional energy around them. With weak, poor or no shields, an empath experiences the emotions of everyone she comes in contact with as her own, whether she wants to or not. As an example, if you're a poorly shielded empath, you may feel absolutely fine, but if an angry person comes into the room, all at once you'll find yourself feeling more and more angry **for no noticeable reason,** even if that person doesn't say a word to you or have any direct interaction with you at all.

This kind of uncontrolled experience can be overwhelming. It can even make you feel a bit crazy. What's worse, other people won't understand you because you're reacting to things they aren't experiencing themselves.

This is why an empath needs good energetic shields.

Good shields keep the emotional energy of others safely outside of your energetic field, and keep your emotional energy safely inside of your field. They let you perceive the difference between your own emotions and the emotions you receive energetically from another person. (I like to think of it as the difference between "mine" and "thine".) They let you receive the information that emotional energy gives you without the necessity of taking it into your body and experiencing it as your own emotions.

Let's talk about how to tweak the basic energetic shields so they more specifically meet an empath's needs.

We talked about combining intention with visualizing light to build basic personal shields. These shields are designed to insulate and protect you from energy from outside of your energetic field, negative energy in particular.

An empath without shields experiences feelings and emotional vibrations around her as if they were her own. She especially needs shields that keep her emotional energy separate and distinct from that of those around her so she's not overwhelmed by energy around her, can function as an individual and can use her gift, rather than be used by it.

If you're an empath and you want to be able to use your gift, you need shields that let you perceive emotional energy without actually taking it into you and experiencing it as your own. To do this, start with the basic technique we went over earlier in this chapter (Need to review? Go ahead- I'll wait...).

As you picture the light around you, set your intention so that your shields only let emotional energy actually touch you if you consciously chose to let it do so. Make it your intention that any emotional energy that you do not chose to let in will stop at the outside edge of your shields. (I tend to think of it as being like a bug on a windshield.) Picture that you'll be able to perceive the information that energy has to give you without taking it into yourself, or experiencing it as your own feelings and becoming overwhelmed.

Over time, your shields will become strong but flexible, able to give you the coverage you need in any circumstance, without cutting you off from the benefits of psychic empathy.

Pretty cool, that. And all for the cost of a little focused daydreaming...

In this chapter, we've gone through some basic information on shielding and why it's important to have good shields. We've gone through ways to develop different levels and types of shields

It's important to know that, while this is useful and practical information, these are not the only ways to develop shields or to work with them. You may learn other information about energetic shielding. You may come up with different images that work better for your personal needs.

That's fine. It's not a one size fits all universe and what works for you is what works for you

You can picture shields as light, or walls, or a personal stronghold. You can build different types of shields and set intentions that make it easy to adjust to different situations. The important thing is to find techniques that help you to keep your energy separate from other energy, so you can stay centered, make good decisions and decide what energy you want to let into your
field and what you do not.

You need control of your energy, and shields help you to gain that control. I'd recommend that you stop reading long enough to start work on developing those shields. I'll be right here waiting for you.

In the next section, we'll be talking about what you do after you create an energetic safe space for yourself.

We'll be talking about clearing out negative energy and the beliefs that help support it.
    See you there.

Clearing Negative Energy

Chapter Five
Grounding Unwanted Energy

Now that we've talked about how to protect our own energy fields, let's talk about unwanted energy and how to clear what we're already carrying. Unwanted energy can be negative energy that drags our vibrations downwards and attracts more negative experiences. It can also be excessive energy that overstimulates us and can have a negative effect on our health and ability to function.

When we're talking clearing unwanted energy that we're already carrying, the best way to do it is by grounding. There are two kinds of grounding in metaphysics

- One is connecting energy to the Earth, in order to increase your ability to manage the energy present and to function effectively.
- The other is using that connection to the Earth to release negative or unwanted energy.

Let's talk about both kinds of grounding.

The first type of grounding strengthens your connection with the physical world.

When you do a lot of metaphysical activity, you'll find a point where you start to get unfocused or vague. (How much is a "lot" varies, dependent on the person, and the conditions prevailing.) You may get dizzy, start to slur your words or have problems making simple decisions (among other things.)

At this point, you're poorly grounded. Processing more magick/ psychic/ metaphysical energy than your body is able to handle at the moment has made your energetic connection with the Earth and physical things (including your body) weaker; and interfered with your ability to function effectively in physical space.

Grounding can strengthen that connection, enabling you to function well again, whether physically or metaphysically.

The second type of grounding is about using your connection with the Earth to release unwanted energy. This may be negative energy but it can also be excess energy that's overwhelming.

Even if you have great shields, sometimes you'll end up picking up someone else's negative energy. For that matter, everyone has times where they generate their own negative energy. (Had a bad hair day lately?) You may feel cranky or irritable or like crying for no good reason. You may overreact to things. You may feel like you have the flu. Negative energy can limit your ability to do things, mess with your health and attract negative experiences (since like calls to like.) If you've got some, it's best to get rid of it.

Grounding is a way of getting rid of negative or unwanted energy. Adding the intention that Mother Earth will recycle it into something positive can yield benefits for all. As an example, in an electrical circuit many outlets have a third hole to hold the third prong on your electrical plug. This arrangement will drain or "ground out" excess energy, preventing harm to appliances or the electrical system. Metaphysical grounding works kind of like that.

There are lots of different ways to ground, and we're going to go over some of them in this chapter.

If you've been working metaphysically with a whole bunch of energy and are starting to feel a bit spacey, one of the best ways to ground your personal energy is physical activity.

Some options:

- Put both of your feet flat on the ground.

- Breathe deeply.
- Stretch. (Take your cue from how a cat stretches.)
- Get up and walk around.
- Clap your hands.
- Stomp your feet.
- Do jumping jacks.
- Dance (Dance hard!)

When you do something physical, you strengthen your connection with your body and the physical world around you. This helps you function better in that physical world.

When choosing physical activity to ground your personal energy, there are a couple of factors to consider.

- If you're poorly grounded, this can affect your alertness, balance and co-ordination. You may wish to start activities involving vigorous movement slowly, to prevent falling.
- When choosing a grounding activity, it's also good to consider your surroundings. In some settings, dancing or jumping jacks may startle or alarm the people around you.

Just remember that, when you're less than grounded, your body has lots of ways to re-establish those energetic connections.

We've talked about using physical activity for grounding and what kind of activities would be good for that). On a related topic, let's talk about food and grounding.

For most of us, eating or drinking is intrinsically grounding of our personal energy. It's a physical activity that involves the physical senses. and tends to strengthen the connections between you and your physical body. (I like to say that eating chocolate pulls me back into body because that's where my tongue is.)

Foods that are particularly grounding include fatty foods (including butter), meat (especially red meat), sugary foods, caffeine and my personal favorite, chocolate.

Now some folks say that, because these kinds of foods are grounding, they're counterproductive if you're doing psychic or metaphysical work. Their concept is kind of like that of a hot-air balloon, with grounding foods serving like weight that prevents lift and taking off. These people tend to feel that, if you're doing metaphysical / psychic work, you should be on a vegetarian diet and be caffeine free.

I respect this theory, but I don't find it true for me. I find that when I'm doing metaphysical / psychic work (especially a lot of such work), I tend to become poorly grounded, and my connections with the physical world become weaker. Amongst other things, this can make it harder for me to talk clearly, and to think of the best words to say to express what I'm "seeing." I'm sure you can see that could be a problem.

I believe that we need to be both grounded and spiritually connected to function at our best. Because of this, when I'm working, I'll have grounding foods and liquids readily available, and eat or drink as needed to keep myself in the best balance between Heaven and Earth possible. (The therapeutic administration of chocolate! What fun!)

Your results may vary.

- You may need that ongoing balance through grounding foods like I do;
- You may only want to use food to ground after you've finished working;
- You may choose to not have grounding food or drink at all around times when you'll be working;
- You may even choose to go caffeine-free or vegetarian in your life-style, to strengthen that esoteric bond.

As always, you have Free Will and the choice is yours. Having the information, I'd encourage you to test it yourself and make your own personal choice about what feels best for you personally.

Food, drink, physical activity; there are so many ways to ground! What's next?

How about a little water to wash everything down with?

In magick and metaphysical work, you're (in effect) shaping the nature of reality using thought, belief, energy and your will. Because of this, thoughts and concepts are powerful tools when working with energy. There's a saying "the symbol is the thing". That means that something that's a symbol of something else can be used to affect that other thing.

Symbolically, water is strong and powerful. It's fluid and flexible. It's very near unstoppable. (Ever try to fix a leak in your basement?) In the context of grounding, we're going to tap into water as the master cleanser. Water is very useful for clearing energy you no longer wish to carry, whether your own energy or energy which has come from outside of you. You can use it to clear cranky or negative emotions, outgrown or dysfunctional beliefs, excess energy, feelings of overwhelm after coming through a crisis, and much, much more.

In the simplest form, you can ground out energy (outside energy or your own) by combining two things:

- water (real or visualized), and
- your intention for the water to carry away energy you do not want or no longer need. (This works well for current issues <u>and</u> long-term problems.)

Some ways to do this?

- If you shook hands with someone who feels untrustworthy (like they "slimed" you?) Wash your hands with the intention that you're cleared of any negative attachments.
- Had a challenging series of encounters with people just this side of hysteria and beginning to feel a little hysterical yourself? Climb into the shower and picture the water carrying the stress of the day away.
- Had someone yelling at you at work and don't have immediate access to water? Close your eyes and picture an energetic waterfall passing over and through you, clearing you of bad vibes.

You get the idea...

It's important when you do this to include in your intention that all negative energy will be cleansed, recycled or otherwise transformed for the highest good of all concerned. You don't want no free-roaming negativity out and about.

Just remember- when it comes to grounding, water is your friend. Go with the flow...

One more classic way of grounding- the Heaven and Earth meditation, which both connects us with the Earth and helps us to use that connection to clear unwanted energy.

Start by finding a time and place when you can meditate without interruptions. Unplug the phone, send your loved ones to the movies and arrange for silence or gentle background music, whichever helps you focus better.

Sit in a comfortable position, with your arms and legs uncrossed and feet flat on the floor. Close your eyes and get ready to meditate.

Take a deep breath and exhale. As you breath out, exhale all tightness and tension in your body. Repeat until you feel your body starting to relax.

There are energy vortexes (called chakras) in many places on your body. Picture the chakras on the soles of your feet and the base of your spine gently opening and energetic roots growing out of them, reaching downwards, downwards until they reach the center of the Earth, and firmly take root there.

And you are firmly grounded and secured to Mother Earth…

There is also a chakra on the crown of your head, just as there are chakras on the soles of your feet and the base of your spine. Picture that chakra gently opening. Picture branches, like the branches of a tree made of light opening out from your crown chakra, spreading gradually as they reach up into the Heavens. Picture those branches spiraling upwards and outwards until they connect with the stars, the moon, the celestial energy that fills the Heavens. Picture that connection being strong and secure, as is your connection with the Earth.

And you are firmly and safely connected between Heaven and Earth

And now we have roots of light, anchoring us to the core of the Earth, and we have branches of light, securing us to the Heavens, and we are suspended safely between Heaven and Earth.

Picture a tunnel of light, a passage through the center of you that connects the chakras at the soles of your feet, the base of your spine and the crown of your head. A
path where light passes freely through you.

Your other five major chakras lie along this path. You can find them:

- just below your navel;
- at your solar plexus;
- at your heart;
- at the base of your throat; and
- between your eyebrows, at your third eye.

Picture these chakras as spinning vortexes, bright and vibrant, full of light and functioning perfectly.

We have roots that reach to the core of the Earth; we have branches that stretch to the Heavens; and now it's time to bring Heaven and Earth together…

Reach down through your roots, down to the energy at the Earth's core. Connect with that energy.

As you breathe, picture that, with every breath, you draw that energy up from the Earth and through your chakras, clearing blockages and energizing yourself as you do so. Continue to breath up the energy from the Earth's core until you feel it reach your crown chakra and rise from it like a fountain.

Reach up through your branches, up to the energy of the Heavens. Connect with that energy.

As you breathe, picture that, with every breath, you draw that energy down from the Heavens and through your chakras, clearing blockages and energizing yourself as you do so.

Continue to breathe the energy from the Heavens until it passes through all of your chakras and out of the ones in your feet. Continue to breathe, feeling the energy of Heaven and Earth filling you, grounding you, clearing you of blockages, energizing you and stabilizing your energy.

If you have any negative or outgrown energy, you can breathe it down into the Earth. Set the intention that it will be recycled and transformed into something positive for the highest good of all concerned. (Mother Earth is powerful, and She's the original recycler!)

Breath until you feel grounded, cleared and in good shape. Then open your eyes.

There are lots of other ways of grounding out negative energy, but now you have three good methods to start with. (There's another grounding visualization in the appendix at the end of this book.) Please try them all and then use the one that suits you best on a regular basis, so you're not carrying around a lot of negative or unwanted energy with you.

We've created a safe space for ourselves energetically by shielding our personal energy. We've cleared out negative energy by grounding, whether it's unwanted energy we got from others or negative energy we've created ourselves.

Clearing negative energy is only part of the process. We all have beliefs, conscious and unconscious, that affect the choices that we make and shape the nature of reality around us. Some of our beliefs are positive and help us to do great deeds and cope with the challenges we face in interesting times. Some were good at one point but we may have outgrown them or they no longer work well for the changing situations around us. Some are negative and can limit or harm us. In the next chapter, we'll be looking at beliefs that are limiting, outgrown or negative, and how to clear them out of our lives.

See you there.

Chapter Six
Clearing Your Mind

Now that we've protected our personal energy and cleared it of unwanted energy, let's start looking at things that can contribute to the kind of energy we create for ourselves. Let's look at our thoughts.

Thoughts are useful tools. When we're stressed, depressed or in a negative energy state, our thoughts can make things better or can make things worse. Thoughts can strengthen a downwards cycle or pull us back up and out of it. Thoughts can empower us or put us into victim mode. Thoughts can help us find solutions to the challenges we face or lock us into those challenges without a way out.

One of the more dysfunctional things that can happen when we're in a negative state is that our thoughts can lock onto our problems and go round and round without bringing us to any solutions. Repeated negative thoughts can drag us into stress, hysteria and depression.

What can we do about a negative mindset? One of the better approaches is meditation. Meditation is a collection of ways to clear and calm our minds, regain our centers, focus on what we want to focus on and break out of the cycle of negativity. It puts us in a better place to make good decisions and move our lives into a better space. Studies find that it also supports health in body, mind and spirit, which is a great bonus.

And it's not that hard to learn or to do.

Some people are concerned that meditation will require a lot of time. "I'm already stressed from all the things I have to do!" they say, "so how do I find the time to do one more thing?!?"

Relax. While longer periods of meditation can have major benefits, studies find that little mini meditations (as short as 3-5 minutes) scattered throughout your day can have benefits like decreasing stress, dropping your blood pressure, boosting your immune system and helping you to be calmer, happier and more focused.

Who knew?

So take a moment for focused breathing, turn your snack into a focused meditation or do a relaxation when you get up from your desk. Mini meditations can improve your energy and help you to have a better day without demanding much of you, and that's a good thing.

Before we get into some specific meditations, let's start by talking about distracting thoughts. In everyday life, our thoughts are racing most of the time. This's particularly true if you multi-task. You're always thinking three steps ahead and your head is full of what you're doing, what you're going to be doing and the two steps in between (and don't get me started on thoughts of the past coming drifting in as well…)

Your mind is usually chattering. Some meditation practices even refer to this as "monkey mind" (with good reason.) Meditation is supposed to calm the "monkey mind"- give us a space when we're not constantly thinking. A rest for the mind. This is one of the reasons that it's so restful and soothing.

That's not always easy. If you're used to your mind chattering all of the time, it won't always stop because you tell it to. You may try to meditate – to soothe your mind and smooth out your chi; and then these darn thoughts keep interrupting you, like demanding little children tugging at the skirts of your psyche.

- What am I having for dinner tonight?
- Is my partner mad at me?
- And my personal favorite - "Gosh, I'm getting good at meditation and focusing only on my breath!"
- "DRAT! I just lost my focus congratulating myself! I'm so bad at this!"
- "DRAT! I'm still distracting myself from my focus!"
- "DRAT! There I go again!"

And so on. You can distract yourself pretty well by beating yourself up for being distracted.

So, how do we deal with monkey mind?

You can't fight those thoughts. If you try to push them away or not think them, you'll trigger resistance, and they'll come back bigger and stronger than before.

- (Don't think about a polar bear!)
- (Did you think about the polar bear? Well, that's the kind of thing I mean…)

Instead, the best response when distracting thoughts intrude is to acknowledge them and tell them not now. Stay calm. Don't beat yourself up for being distracted for a moment. It happens to everyone. Instead think "I see that I'm thinking about Great Aunt Ethel. Fine. I'm now returning my thoughts to my breathing."

And go back to your meditation.

Just let distracting thoughts drift across your mind like clouds across a summer sky and turn back to your meditation again.

Skip the struggle, relax and refocus.

Let's start with one of the most basic meditation

techniques. Let's start with breathing.

Find a time where you're unlikely to be interrupted. Position yourself comfortably, and then just focus on your breath. Feel yourself breathe in, and breathe out, and breathe in again. Keep your attention on your breathing.

This is harder than it sounds. At first, you may find thoughts jumping in to interrupt. We're all so used to multi-tasking that many of us have problems with focusing on one thing at a time (even if it feels good and will do us good).

You may find your list of things to do today, and old grudges, and thoughts like "This is stupid.", "Oops, I got distracted from my breath by thinking. I blew it.", and "Drat, there I am, thinking again!" popping up.

Don't fight these thoughts. That only makes it worse. Just return your focus to your breathing, without judging yourself. You'll find this feels really good after a while. Very restful.

Focus on your breathing for whatever time you have (5 minutes; 10; whatever) then open your eyes, and go forth to face the day.

In modern society, we're constantly on the run. Move, move, move! Multitask, multitask, multitask!
As a consequence, we get a whole lot of stuff done – but we also lose the ability to simply be present with what we're doing at the moment. If you're juggling chain saws, you have to constantly be thinking three steps ahead or bad things will happen.

Maybe so, maybe no. But, we're always thinking too fast and too far, and that can just wear you out.

One form of meditation is simply being totally present with what you are now. Putting plans, and multitasking, and thinking ahead aside for a little while and really being there in the moment with what you're doing, whether chanting, or exercising, or playing with your child. The act of presence helps to still the chatter of the monkey mind, and build an inner calm, which is very pleasant, relaxing, and healing.

One good time to do it is while eating. Chose a time and place for your eating meditation where you won't be interrupted. Turn off phones, and position yourself where folks won't come by every few seconds wanting to chat or for you to find their lost sneaker.

Chose an item of food to focus on. An orange or apple is traditional, but you can do this with any type of food, even a cookie or a hamburger. Put aside any worries, planning, or thinking about the next three things on your to-do list. This is just a little meditation, and all of those things will be there when you get back.

Start by focusing on the food you in your hand. What does it feel like?

- Is it heavy or light? How heavy?
- What is its texture?
- Is it hard, or soft? If soft, try "squishing" it a bit, to see what that feels like.

Look at your food. Turn it around, so you can look at it from all sides. What does it look like?

- What color is it?
- Is it a solid color or does it have variations?
- Look closely at it. Would you would be able to pick it out from others of its type?

How about sound? Is your food

- Crispy like a chip?
- Crunchy like good french bread?
- Thumpable, like a melon?

Bring your food to your nose, and smell it. Is the smell

- Sweet?
- Tangy?
- Rich?
- Bland?

Now finally, it's time to taste. Take a small nibble of your food and hold it in your mouth for a moment, really focusing on the flavor and how it feels on your tongue. Start to chew, and notice how the experience changes for you. Spend as little or as much time being present with your food as you like.

If distracting thoughts come up, your planning mind tries to play through and the monkey mind begins to chatter, you already know how to deal with that. Return to your food meditation until you're ready to end it

The more deeply you focus on your food, the more that you tune into the sensory experiences your food has to give you, the more your mind will calm and your stress will lessen. Not only is meditation good for your health in general, but a food mindfulness meditation like this one can also help develop better eating habits, which can help with indigestion and being overweight.

So, enjoy your mindfulness snack, and have a better day.

Because we live in a busy multitasking, "six impossible things before breakfast" kind of world, we tend to build up a lot of tension. Many times, that tension settles in our muscles and joints. The jaw. The neck. The shoulders. The back. Any part that's a part of you can get tense and tight and painful because you're stressed. Meditation, even for a few minutes, can help with that.

Pick a time when you'll be free from interruptions

for a few minutes. (Hide in the bathroom, or in your car is you need to.) Put yourself in a comfortable position, sitting or lying, with your arms and legs uncrossed (so they won't go to sleep.) Close your eyes.

Start by doing some relaxing deep breathing. As you feel your body start to relax, gently focus on the different parts of your body, starting with your toes and working your way upwards.

Where are you holding your tension? Your neck? Your back? When you find a part of your body that's tense, stop there and breath. Picture yourself breathing light into that part of the body – light that fills it, heals it and lets it relax.

Be aware of that part of you as it relaxes. See how good it feels? That's how it's supposed to feel. Make a note of this, so that, the next time it starts to get tense, you'll be aware of it, and know you need to do some more relaxation

Once that part of your body relaxes, move on to the rest of it; and, when your time is up and your body is relaxed, open your eyes.

This is a simple but very effective technique. You can do your whole body, or, if you've only got a minute or two, you can focus on the parts of your body where you know you tend to carry tension. Either way, it's good for your head and good for your body as well. (Tense muscles are more vulnerable to injury).

One other way of meditating is the practice of prayer. Prayer in any form helps to still the mind, bring our focus back to what is positive and what we hope for, and gives us a way to connect with the Divine, in whatever way we believe, in order to ask for inspiration, help and support.

Whether you work with prayers of gratitude, prayers of intercession for others, or prayers of petition for help for yourself, a prayer practice is a powerful tool, especially if you do it on a regular basis.

There are lots of other ways to meditate. (You can find three more meditations in the appendix at the end of this book.) Some take minutes and others take longer but they're all good for you and will help your energy by helping you to clear negative thoughts. The question is more finding the meditation that works for you and then doing it on a regular basis.

Meditation helps to clear the chatter, the thoughts that distract us from what's going on and the ones that pull us downwards. Next let's look at our thoughts and beliefs and how they affect how we interact with the world.

Chapter Seven
Mind the Gap

It's important to still your mind and end the mental chatter so you can find your center and deal with what's happening. By itself, it's not enough, though.

Once we get past the immediate chatter, we need to take a good look at our thoughts and beliefs, both conscious and unconscious. Some of those beliefs will serve us well. Some not so well- and some are just messing with us.

That affects how we see the world around us and interact with it.

Let's take a look at our beliefs and how they work in our lives.

It used to be that social scientists thought everything was stimulus/response. Something happened, you reacted to it, and life went on from there.

But when they started looking more closely at things, they found something different and interesting.

The world was not made up of stimulus and response. Stimulus and response happen, it's true, but in between the two of them is a little gap, and it's what happens in the gap that sets the tone for your life.

The stimulus/ response reaction actually has three parts not two.

- First something happens- the stimulus.
- Next comes the gap between stimulus and response. In that gap, the person reacting attaches a meaning to what has just happened.
- And finally, the person reacts, based less on the stimulus and more on what they believe about that

stimulus.

Hmm.
That's why a hundred people can have the same experience, and still come away with different reactions to it. They're reacting to the meaning they've attached to the stimulus in the gap- to the stories they have told themselves about the experience.
This is a useful thing to know.

We gain more control of our situation by taking a look at what is going on in the gap- what beliefs we live by, what mental tendencies we have.
Do you believe:

- There always is an answer, so all you have to do is look for it?
- Bad things always happen to you?
- People are good if you give them a chance?
- That you're lucky?
- Everything happens for a reason?

We all have general settings for our emotions and general beliefs that we see the world by. Some of those beliefs may be helpful to us, and some of them may be not. The interesting thing is that there are ways we can change that belief default setting of to support better energy and a better life.
It's worth taking a good hard look at your beliefs about the world. What types of meanings do you tend to apply to your experiences? What stories do you tell yourself about yourself and your life?

Recurring events. Going through the same experience over and over, either with the same partners or different people every time

If the experience is good, keep going; but if you find yourself replaying the same unpleasant routines over and over, it's worth looking at what's going on in the gap that might be keeping you going around in circles.

- Is there something you were supposed to learn from the situation but haven't?
- Have you learned a belief that creates more bad situations? (ex: one bad romantic experience leads you to believe that you need to protect yourself from every partner…)
- Do you expect bad things to happen? (i.e. "…bad things always happen to me…")

If you find that you have a recurring negative situation, it's good to stop and look at what kinds of beliefs might be contributing to it. You can't control everyone else, but your own beliefs and reactions are something that you can change, and that gives you the chance to break out of a negative pattern.

Truth. In some situations, there is only one truth; but many situations contain an assortment of responses that are all true.

- As an example, I'm allergic to oranges, but that doesn't mean that oranges are unhealthy for everyone. It means that they're healthy for most people and unhealthy for me, and both of those things are true.

- As another example, you may want to help someone you love to do something in order to make things easier or save them pain. Your loved one may want or need to do the hard thing themselves because it is something they need to learn or accomplish so they can learn and grow. Make things easy and learning the hard stuff are both truths, but which one is more important depends on who you are.

As I've said before, some truths will serve you better than others, so if you're looking at a situation with multiple truths, why not choose the one that is in keeping with your values but that serves you better?

If your energy is low, or things aren't working out well, stop, look and think.

- Is this the only truth in my situation?
- Are there other ways to see this that are also true?
- Am I making this harder or more negative for myself than I have to?
- Is there a better way to see this?

Many times, we're so fixed on the option right in front of us that we miss the fact that there are other options that may satisfy our values but give us better results. When things aren't working, it's good to look and see if you're missing other options.

When you get on an English train or subway, there's often a sign that says "Mind the gap." to keep you from tripping or losing things. It's even more important to mind the gap in life in general - to examine the meanings you attach to people, things and experiences, and to question the beliefs you have that affect how you see the world and interact with it.

Choose truth. Choose beliefs that align with your values- but look at the beliefs you're using as your operating system and ask yourself whether these are the best truths that you can carry around with you. If they are, great. If not, we'll be looking later in this book at some ways to let go of dysfunctional beliefs and replace them with ones that serve you better.

For now, it's enough to know that those beliefs are there, that they can make a difference between a life that is positive and productive and one that's not, and that there are ways to change the beliefs that don't serve you well.

And now that we've cleared the chatter and looked more closely at our thoughts and beliefs, the next step is to become more aware of our energy and the energy of the world around us- and that's in the next section. See you there

Being More Aware

Chapter Eight
Noticing What's Happening

You've learned some basics of how energy works and how to protect your personal energy through shielding. You've learned about clearing out negative energy. You've learned how to calm your mind and clear it of outgrown, dysfunctional or negative beliefs that shape your choices and the nature of reality around you

Hopefully, you've taken some basic steps to protect your energy, to clear out negative and unwanted energy and to clear your mind. If you haven't, please stop and do it now.

Why am I asking you to do this first? If you're constantly being assailed by outside stress, anger, fear, resentment and other kinds of negative energy, it's a lot harder to think straight. It's harder to learn things and make good decisions and just plain focus. It's harder to find your center when the winds of challenging times are blowing.

Please take a moment to start working on your own energetic shelter now, so you'll be in a better space to add on other methods to help yourself and others.

Go ahead. I'll wait…

OK- now that you've built space to shelter you against outside energy, let's move on to the next step – awareness.

Many times, stress and negative energy sneaks up on us. We don't notice how bad it's getting right up to the point where it becomes overwhelming. By then, it's hard to manage.

There's an old story that says if you drop a frog into a pot of boiling water, he will struggle and hop and do everything he can to escape, but if you put him in a pot of cold water and gradually raise the temperature, he'll just adapt until he boils to death.

Ugh. Nasty story- but it's a good illustration of how many of us deal with stress and negative energy. It starts small and we think "I can handle this..." and it gradually piles up until it buries us under a pile of misery because we don't notice that it's gradually increasing. If we pay more attention, if we become more aware of the signs that negative energy is building up in our lives, it's easier to manage or eliminate that energy and we have a better chance of doing so before that energy can do damage.

So how do we become aware of negative energy so we can address it? Well, it starts with our bodies...

Your body is talking to you. It's trying to let you know when you're off center, out of balance or spiraling out of control. If you listen to it, you can take control of your energy before it's stressed or overwhelmed.

How do you hear what it's trying to tell you? A good start is knowing how your body feels when you're functioning like you usually do.

Not everyone has the same energy levels. Not everyone has the same default setting, so it's important to know what's normal for you. While you want to get your vibration as high as you can and keep it there as much as possible, knowing the level you start out at helps you to notice if things are not working the way you want them to, so you can do something about it.

So, as the philosophers say, the first step is to know yourself.

The next step is to know what your body feels like when it's stressed. Stress hits different people in different parts of the body. It can show up in places like your

- Forehead,
- Temples,
- Jaw,
- Neck,
- Shoulders,
- Back,
- Or any other place that tends to hurt.

Stress can show up as aches, pain, stiffness, congestion or other types of pain or dysfunction. My stress tends to hit me in the jaw, the neck, the shoulders and my lower back. Where does yours hit?

Stress can also show up as illness or injury too. If you find you're:

- Tripping and falling more,
- Having more headaches,
- Catching more or worse colds,
- Feeling tired more easily,

These are all also signs of possible negative energy. Sometimes a cold is just a cold, but, when you're stressed or overwhelmed with negative energy, your immune system cannot work as well, and you may find you have more health problems.

If you're having more neck pain, or tripping and falling more, or getting sick more, or are always tired, it's a good thing to stop and pay attention to what's happening and whether you need to take care of your own energy.

Is it just a health issue, or do you need to manage your energy so your body can manage your health?

In addition to listening to your body, it's also a good idea to listen to your emotions, because they also can give us cues to things that drop our energy into negative levels.

Is there a person or activity that makes you feel afraid or that you have a negative response to? Sometimes that's an alert to things or people or activities that drain your energy or that flood you with negative energy.

We all have activities we don't like that we nonetheless have to deal with. (Changing diapers, doing taxes, and being with certain people leaps to mind...) Some of these are just things we don't like to do. Some of them are sources of negative energy. Being aware of who and what these are lets us be prepared for the possibility. It can also let find ways to limit, control or otherwise manage those experiences. (For example, if you don't like doing your taxes and accountant B gives you the creeps, hire accountant A...)

People tell you to be logical and not to get overly emotional. I'd say that your brain has both a logical side and a feeling side for a reason, and listening to both can give you useful information about when your energy is in a healthy space and when you need to do some work on it.

Finally, it's good to listen to your dreams. Dreams are one way that our inner wisdom tells us things our conscious mind isn't aware of, or that we've been avoiding looking at. Sometimes dreams are just your mind playing around or signs of illness, but sometimes dreams are your unconscious minds way of giving you information.

Sometimes dreams are literal. You dream about the car not starting, and the following day, the car doesn't start. Sometimes dreams are symbolic. You dream about walking down the street naked and the next day, you have an embarrassing experience. And sometimes dreams are psychic, and give you information you weren't getting with your five senses.

If you have a dream that seems particularly intense, particularly real or particularly important, take a moment to see if it has a message for you.

- Write down everything you remember about the dream.
- Mark the elements (people, items, animals, actions) that stick out at you.
- Ask yourself "what does this element mean to me? and "how did this element make me feel?"
- Then see if you start to get the message the dream was trying to give you.

Listen to your dreams. They can sometimes give you information you won't get in any other way.

If you want to know if your energy is in balance, or if you need to do something to bring yourself back to center, you need to start by being aware.

Listen to your body.

Listen to your emotions.

Listen to your dreams.

And take the information you get to know what helps you and what drains you. Once you know that, you can move forwards towards more positive energy and a happier life.

Chapter Nine
Know What Drains You

In the last chapter, we talked about being aware of when you're stressed and overwhelmed, and when your vibrations are dropping into the lower levels. We talked about different signs to watch for to tell you that this is happening.

Now that we know how to identify this, it's time to look at identifying what's taking your energy down, so that you can deal with it.

The first step is to know what your normal energy levels are. Some of us are naturally high energy and some of us have to work at it. Some of us have chronic conditions, such as depression or chronic pain, that sap our energy. It's important to know what your standard energy levels are, because it makes it easier to notice when your energy levels start to slip

It's also important to be able to evaluate your current situation, so you can tell the difference between a short time dip in your energy and something more serious.

There's a difference between being down and having depression. There's a difference between being exhausted because you're short of sleep and because you're wrestling with a chronic disease. Knowing what your standard energy levels are can tip you off if your energy levels start to slip. It gives you the chance to do something about it before the problem gets worse in both short time
situations and long term ones (and that can be helpful.)

Your body is talking to you.
In the last chapter, we talked about how your body

is talking to you. How aches and pains, illness and accidents are sometimes just aches and pains, illness and accidents, but sometimes they're your body's way of letting you know that your vibrational level is dropping and that you need to do something about it.

If you used the information in the last chapter then you probably have a pretty good list of where stress and negative energy hit you.

Do you:

- Start having aches and pains more?
- Feel like it's all too much/ more than you can handle?
- Feel like you're coming down with a cold?
- Get more emotional, especially negative emotions?
- Feel like you're more clumsy?
- Even start having more close calls or even accidents?

These are wake-up calls to let you know that your vibrational level is under siege and that it's up to you to do something about it.

It's time to pay attention to your body and your emotions. What are they trying to tell you?

Sometimes a cold is just a cold. Sometimes a bad mood is just a bad mood- but sometimes they're alerts to let you know that you're overworked, over stressed or heading into more negative energy.

How do you tell the difference?

Look at the circumstances surrounding you.

- Out of nowhere, you find yourself coming down with a cold. Is it the cold and flu season? Do other people around you have colds? Do you come in contact with

someone who's more likely to carry a cold? (ex: Do you have a child in daycare?)
- You find yourself in a really bad mood. Has something negative or frustrating happened? Is your mood in balance with what's happening around you, or does it seem much worse than the actual situation would indicate?

Illness, injury, excessive emotional reactions or negative feelings that come out of nowhere can often be indicators that there is something else going on at an energetic level. If you're experiencing these things, it's good to sit back and evaluate what's going on. Figure out if you've been exposed to something you associate with past trauma, you're just having a bad day, or whether you're being sabotaged or overwhelmed by unwanted, negative or excess energy.

If you think that you've got negative energy in play, it's time to see if you can figure out where it's coming from. Is it:

- Negative people?
- Too much stress?
- Not enough sleep?
- Dehydration?
- Not enough of the kinds of foods your body wants?
- Needy people?
- Chronic pain?
- Trying to do too much and getting overwhelmed?
- Neglecting your own wellbeing/
- Any combination of factors like these?

It's also worth noting that symptoms can come from an assortment of factors, some physical (such as allergies), some mental or emotional (such as stress) and some energetic (such as other people's emotional energy or old experiences you're still carrying with you.) As human beings, we're complicated, and that can sometimes make it hard to narrow down where those "out of nowhere" blues or pattern of things falling apart are coming from.

Sometimes to figure things out, you need to try things one by one and see what makes a difference. An energy journal can help with this.

Start by using a notebook to keep track of those days when things just go wrong for no reason. You can include things like

- The out of the usual negative experiences you have.
- What the weather was like.
- If you'd gotten enough sleep.
- If other people are experiencing the same thing around you.
- Things you'd eaten.
- People you'd spent time with
- Things like that.

Once you've written down several situations, start looking for common elements. Do you

- Get tired or achy when a storm is coming in?
- Feel angry or scared when you have too much on your to do list?
- Feel cranky or stressed when you spend time with certain people?

Once you've got a list of possible things, people or experiences that drain your energy, try limiting or eliminating them one by one, and see what makes a difference for you.

There's lots of different things that can start your energy on a downward spiral. Identifying the ones that tend to drain you is an important step in getting control of your own energy back.

It's worth noting that not everything that drains your energy is strictly energetic. Ongoing illness or injury or overwhelming circumstances can also cause an energetic drain if you live with them long term. Things in the physical world like:

- Chronic pain.
- Physical limitations.
- Chronic depression.
- Ongoing bullying or intimidation.
- Working multiple jobs.
- Family crisis.

They're all things happening in the physical world that can still cause energetic drain if we're living with them long enough. It's good to try to identify things that drain you in the physical world as well as the energetic one.

There's lots of different people and things and experiences that can drain or overwhelm you. Since it's not a "one size fits everyone" universe, the things that send us into a negative spiral are different for everyone. That's why identifying the ones that tend to drain you is the next step to learning how to survive and thrive in interesting times.

Sit back. Center yourself. And then see if you can spot the people, things and experiences that have a negative effect on your energy.

In the next few chapters, we'll look at how to deal with them once we've spotted them.

Chapter Ten
Stop the Drain

We've looked at knowing when our energy is dropping lower and at identifying things and people and activities that contribute to that. Now let's look at what we can do in response.

First and foremost, we can just say no. Say no to the things that we know drain us or depress us.

Now many of you are going to say "I can't stop doing things just because they drain my energy or bring my vibration lower." In some cases, that's true, but in many cases, we're doing things because we think we have to, and that may not actually be the situation.

Some things you really have to do.

- Make a living.
- Drink enough water so that you don't get dehydrated.
- Brush your teeth.
- Feed your children and your pets.

Many other things fall into the category of "the dreaded shoulds.". We're told we should do these things but we may not actually have to.

- We should recycle.
- We should get involved in politics.
- We should be well informed about everything.
- We should save the environment.

In these cases, "should" is code for "it would be

really nice if you could do these things"- and the tricky part is that nobody can do all of them. Nobody.

The first step is looking at all of the things that drain you or deplete your energy and decide which ones really need to get done and which ones you can let go of, temporarily or permanently.

Then let them go. Say no. No thank you. Not now. Not ever. It isn't always easy, but it's an important part of cutting your stress and getting your life back.

Notice how many times your energy feels better almost immediately with that weight off your shoulders…

We've started by saying no to the things that drain or depress us, and that don't have to be in our lives. The next step is looking at the things that do have to get done and prioritizing them.

- Do you have to do this?
- Do you have to do this in the way you've been doing it?
- Is there a way to do it that's more positive/ more fun/ that'll be better for your energy?
- Do you have to do this as often as you have been doing it?
- Do <u>you</u> have to do it? Can you simplify it/order it/ delegate it/ hire someone?
- Is there someone in your life who enjoys doing this and would do this for you if you did one of their chores that you enjoy?

If there are things that have to get done, it doesn't mean that you have to do them, that they have to get done every day, that you can't find a better way to get them done. Think of things like:

- Putting on music you love when you do the housekeeping.
- Swopping child care with a friend who also has kids, to give you time for other things.
- Cutting back how often you mow the lawn.
- Getting take out if you're too tired to cook one night.

Think about what needs to get done, and whether you can make it more pleasant/ less labor intensive/ less frequent/ or share the load with someone else.

Then use the time you've opened up for something that feeds your spirit rather than drains it.

Social media, t.v. and news can be fun, but they can also be exhausting and draining when you spend too much time with them. (How much is too much depends on the individual and how many other things are going on in your life.) We all want to be informed and we all want to stay in touch, but there are times when we need to sign off or limit contact time to keep our centers.

Whether you're watching or listening to the news or spending time online, be sure to listen to what your body is telling you. If you start having signs of stress or energetic drain, it's time to sign off for a while and do something that builds your energy back up again. If you find you don't notice a problem until you're already overwhelmed, you might start setting a timer to remind you to check your energy before you end up in the doldrums.

Take a break. Don't worry. It'll all be there when you get back.

Some people feed your spirit and make you feel good. Some people don't. Some people are very high maintenance and drain your energy like a vampire with a bendy straw.

That's something to take a good hard look at. It's good to give your time and energy and love to the people who build you up and make you feel better about the world. Those other people, though, the high maintenance people, you should really give some thought to.

Some of them are all take and no give. They may be in your life as a habit- because they're a friend of a friend of a friend or you've been hanging together since third grade, but if you feel rotten every time you have contact with them, maybe it's time to take a break.

Is this a person that belongs in your life? If not, it may be time to be polite but let them go.

Some of these folks may be high maintenance, but people that you still want in your life. If that's the case, you may want to give some thought to how much of your time and energy you want to give them. Maybe you need to cut down on or control your contacts. Maybe you need to call screen. Maybe you need to save contacts for when you're feeling good and can afford to give away some energy, as opposed to being at their beck and call whether or not you're up to it.

If you have someone in your life who's high maintenance and needy, you give them better energy if you do it when your vibrations are high and you're feeling strong, as opposed to letting them drain you dry. That's better for both of you.

Remember, you get to choose who's in your life and how much. It's better to choose people who support your positive energy as opposed to drain you dry.

If you've still got high maintenance people in your life, you may find that you end up having to set boundaries.

- Call screen and don't answer the phone if you're not up to the kind of conversation they typically want.
- Say "I can help you this much and no more so."
- If you're the one doing the favor, you get to choose when and how its most convenient for you to do so.

You may even get to the point where you have to be explicit and tell them that you're not available to do things that they want, or that you can't talk to them if they're not treating you with respect.

Remain calm.

Before you do this, get a clear picture what your boundaries are. Figure out how to state them clearly. Rehearse this.

Then be prepared to say "no", walk away or hang up if they're having problems listening to you. Sometimes boundaries have to be firmly stated before you gain respect for them and for yourself.

Setting boundaries is treating yourself with respect. It's treating the other person with respect, too, because it makes it clear what they can expect from you and what they can't, and works from the idea that, once they know this, you both can build a better relationship.

It supports better energy for both of you, and that's a good thing.

If you burn your hand, you need to stick your hand in cold water as soon as possible. If you don't, the burn will continue to burn until you finally immerse it.

Stress and negative energy are kind of like that. If you hit the point of energetic overwhelm, your vibrations begin to spiral downwards. The further down they go, the more negative you feel and the more negative things you attract. This can take the spiral further down.

What's first aid for this energetic burn? Try shifting your focus.

You'll probably need to give some attention to whatever's bothering you to keep from having further problems, but beyond that, try to give as much attention and energy as you can to what's actually working in your life. Cuddle your dog or cat. Count your blessings. Give or receive hugs.

When we focus on things that are more positive to us, we pull our energy back upwards again; sometimes a little at a time and sometimes more so. By doing this enough, we can break the negative cycle and start to repair what's going wrong.

Are things negative? Do what you can to shift your focus and soothe the negative burn that life has dealt you.

When you're living in interesting times, no matter what you do, there will be times when you get hit by the overwhelm, and your vibrations shoot downwards. For this reason, you need to plan room for recovery time in your life.

In this day and age, we're constantly running place to place, multitasking and trying to cram just "one more thing" into our schedules. Because of this, we often lack the time to stop, take a deep breath, re-center ourselves and overcome any overwhelm.

Plan to do a little less. Leave yourself open time and flexibility in your life, so you can stop and get your center back if you need to. Leave time for serendipity. Leave yourself some wiggle room.

Don't cram your life so full of obligations that you have no time to breath. Leave yourself time to recover- and use it when you need it. We'll be talking about how in coming chapters.

We've looked at what causes negative energy and, in this chapter, we've looked at some ways to limit or stop those things from doing further damage to us. Starting with the next chapter, we're be looking at ways to build ourselves up, as opposed to just keep from dropping down.

See you there.

Building Your Positive Energy

Chapter Eleven
Know What Strengthens You

For every yin, there is a yang. For every down, there is an up. We've talked about what drains your energy and pushes your vibration into negative levels. We've talked about what you can do about that, to stop losing energetic ground or at least limit how much drain you accept.

Now let's talk about the other side of the coin. Let's talk about what feeds you energetically in body, mind and spirit. About what pushes your energy up into higher vibrations. About what heals you as opposed to drains you.

Yes, please- let's have some of that.

Your body is talking to you.

Just as it was telling you when you're getting drained or overwhelmed, your body also tries to tell you when something or someone is good for your energy. It lets you know what things are good for you, so you can make the best use of them and choose to have more of them in your life.

It's good to pay attention, whether your body is alerting you to a negative energetic cycle, or to an upwards surge, and use that information to make your life better.

How do we do that?

What are your signs of your energy increasing? Close your eyes and listen to your body.

You know what it feels like when you're stressed, depressed or coming down with a cold. Sometimes a cold is just a cold, but those sensations can also indicate an energy drain.

Let's flip the coin and remember when we had something good happen to us. Something that filled us with joy or peace or just that "YES!!" feeling

What did it feel like? Some possibilities are

- Feeling happy.
- Feeling relaxed.
- Feeling like a great weight has been lifted off your shoulders.
- Getting giddy or silly.
- Relaxation of muscles in places like your forehead, jaw, neck, shoulders or back.
- Wanting to dance or sing or jump up and down.
- Feeling full of energy.
- Getting a big sappy grin on your face.
- Wanting to share that good feeling with someone else, including total strangers.

Don't just stop with picturing one good experience. Picture as many as you can think of, and note what feelings those experiences have in common. These are the cues that the world is topping off your energetic tank.

There's lots of different ways that you can feel the energy rising higher in you. Since it's not a one size fits all universe, there are no right or wrong answers where this is concerned. The one common theme is that should all feel good- the rest is up to you and your body.

And, once you know what signs you're looking for, the next step is to look for the source.

Where's that positive energy coming from?

Sometimes, we feel good for no perceptible reason. Some undefined combinations of elements in the universe adds up to "a perfect day" and we enjoy it as our energy climbs because of it.

Serendipity rocks, and by all means enjoy it. That being said, if you can figure out what's raising your energy like that, it's a bonus, because it increases the chances that you can **do it again.**

Hopefully, many more times.

Not just because it feels good (although that's certainly reason enough…) but also because the more you feed your energy, the more it stays at a higher vibration. The more it does that, the happier, healthier and more successful you will be in your life in general.

It's worth noting those good feelings for that reason. It's also worth noting the people, activities and situations that tend to be associated with feeling that way.

Good energy can come from people:

- People you know and who care for you.
- People you encounter randomly.
- People you don't interact with, but whose random good vibes do a drive by on your energy.
- People (real or fictional) you read about or see on t.v. or in the movies.
- People who cross your path briefly, but offer the right word or the right action at the right time.

Good energy can come from places:

- A peaceful chapel.
- A lively marketplace.
- A bookstore.
- A place you have good associations with.

Good energy can come from things:

- A delicious cookie.
- The smell of a particular flower.
- A pen that feels right in your hand.
- Comfortable slippers.

Good energy can come from experiences:

- An inspirational movie.
- Singing along with the radio as you drive.
- Watching a child do something for the first time.
- Completing a responsibility and checking it off your "to-do" list.
- A joke that makes you laugh until you cry.

Since we're all unique, the things that feel good and boost our energy are different for every person. There is no wrong answer. The important thing is to pay attention and figure out what things lift your energy upwards. (Bonus style points for figuring out if these things have any common themes. That may make it easier to find other things that will likewise lift you upwards.)

Knowing these things will make it easier for you to keep your energy positive, and that will make it easier to have a better life.

Think about it. What things lift your energy upwards?

Once you know the things that lift your energy upwards, you've got one final step for knowing yourself. I want you to make yourself a list. And I want you to put that list in a place that's easy to find it when you need it.

Why? Well, a list of things that raise your energy upwards is generally useful to keep your energy positive and support the kind of life you want, but you're gonna want it even more when things are blue.

Anybody can have a bad day, and a day when things are awkward/uncomfortable/frustrating/scary can start your energy plummeting down into the lower ranges. At that point, one thing you can do to reverse that plummet is to do things that make you feel good and lift your energy up again.

Unfortunately, when you're frustrated, angry or scared, it's a lot harder to think of things that do work in your life and a lot easier to focus on what's wrong- which feeds the drop. That's where an actual concrete list comes in handy. It shows you things that are positive, even if you can't think of any right now. It reminds you that frustration or fear is not forever and that there are decent things in the future ahead. It helps you to start climbing upwards again, as opposed to just spinning out.

For that reason, it's a good idea to make an actual list. It's also important to keep it in a place where it's easy to get at it. (A list that you can't find does you no good.) You may even want to make several and keep them different places such as

- Your day planner
- Taped up by your mirror
- On your desk

Or wherever else you'll see it easily and often.

Keep in mind that it's o.k. to add to this list as more things come to you (indeed, that's a great idea) and look it over on a regular basis to keep your focus on the positive things in your life.

Just looking at your list can lift your energy- and using it as a reminder to make these things a regular part of your life will help keep your energy at that higher level.

It's good to know the things and people and experiences that drain your energy, so you can control them or let go of them. It's also good to know the things and people and experiences that feed your energy, so that you can use that knowledge to support your health and energy and draw more positive things into your life.

We'll be talking about that in the next chapter…

Chapter Twelve
Make Nurturing Yourself a Priority

In the last chapter, we talked about identifying the people, things and experiences that feed your energy and support you in body, mind, and spirit. Now it's time to talk about doing something with that knowledge and about making nurturing yourself one of your priorities.

Why is nurturing important? There are a number of reasons.

- Being nurtured feels good.
- It's maintenance for you in body, mind and spirit.
- It puts balance back into your life.
- It supports joy and peace, both of which are healthy states.
- It decreases your stress and helps you relax.
- Studies find that it supports a healthy body, mind and spirit.

Everybody needs people, things and experiences that make them feel good and that feed their energy in positive ways. It helps us to be healthy, happy and function better in whatever situation we find ourselves in. Nurturing ourselves is one way to make sure that happens.

Let's look at the process more closely.

It's wonderful when people do things to make us happy or show us that they care about us. Give us hugs. Bring us soup when we're sick. Really listen when we need to talk.

There are reasons though why it's not always a good idea to count on getting all of our nurturing from others.

- People don't always know what kind of nurturing you need.
- Anyone can have a bad day, and forget to nurture the people around them.
- People have lots of obligations and may not always be able to nurture you when you need or want them to.

The bottom line is that people are good and people care, but sometimes they may still not be able to be there for you when you need them. No fault, no blame- that's just how it is sometimes.

The best idea seems to be to take the lead on nurturing yourself and seeing that your own needs are met.

- When you need nurturing, you're already right there.
- You know what you need and when you need it.
- If you're having a bad day, all the more reason to do something nice for yourself.
- You can choose to make your own happiness and well-being one of your priorities as opposed to waiting for someone else to do it for you.

We all need a certain amount of nurturing to stay healthy and happy and keep from burning out. If we make it our own responsibility to be sure that we get that nurturing, the odds are better that it'll happen and anything else we get from others is gravy

So be your own best friend choose to take care of yourself, and have a happier, healthier life.

It's good to be nurtured and to nurture yourself, but there are some beliefs that can get in the way of that happening. We all have conscious and unconscious beliefs that affect our relationship with the world. Some of those beliefs may not work for our best benefit. Some examples of these:

- Perfectionism- Some people will break themselves trying to meet impossible standards.
- Martyrdom- Some people are so busy trying to take care of everyone else that they forget to take care of themselves.
- Guilt- Some people feel like they do not deserve good things happening to them.
- Selfishness- Some people feel guilty about taking the time or effort to nurture themselves. They feel like it's selfish.

These beliefs can start in good places, but if you take them too far, they can become unhealthy and keep you from having the balance you need for a happy, healthy life.

If you have these beliefs, you might want to consider:

- Perspective – You don't have to be perfect. Let good enough be good enough.
- Balance- Remember to put yourself on your own list of people you nurture and take care of.
- Worthiness- Kindness and goodness are not things that you need to earn. Everyone deserves them and you do too, if you'll allow yourself to receive them.
- Health – Nurturing yourself is not a selfish act. It's self maintenance that helps keep you strong and healthy in body, mind, and spirit, and that means

you're in condition to help others. It's a mutual "win-win."

It's good to challenge ideas that can harm you and burn you out. If you have these limiting beliefs, let them go and replace them with beliefs that promote balance, peace and positive energy.

We get out of the habit of taking care of ourselves.

It's not our fault. We're taught to fill our days with as many things as possible- meeting responsibilities, multitasking, doing great deeds, taking care of others and so forth. Somewhere in there, taking care of ourselves gets lost. It's relegated to "when I have time"- and somehow that time doesn't happen.

So, what do you do when you're trying to make time for something? You schedule it.

No really. I know it sounds crazy, but this can make a difference.

Make an appointment to do something nice for yourself. Have a checklist and do a certain number of self-nurturing things a day. For heaven's sake, write the specific experience in your schedule book if you need to.

At one point in my life, I had a chocolate scented lotion that put a grin on my face every time I used it. I was so out of practice with taking care of my own needs that I had to write "hand lotion" in my schedule every day, until I'd built myself a happy habit again.

Now that may sound sad, but truth be told, when you're doing lots of things, these are the kinds of things that get lost unless we find some way to make them visible, and its little things like this can affect the quality of your energy and your life.

Studies find that it takes at least 30 days to build a new habit so that you don't have to concentrate on doing it. Scheduling time to nurture yourself can be a great way of making this a regular part of your life.

Final points?

- Nurturing feels good.
- Nurturing supports balance in your life.
- Nurturing prevents burnout.
- Nurturing yourself is not selfish. It's the maintenance you need to stay strong and healthy, both for your own sake and so that you can help others.
- Nurturing keeps your vibrations in the higher range. That attracts more good people, experiences, and things into your life.
- Nurturing is important to keep you healthy in body mind and spirit.
- Self-nurturing increases the chance that you will consistently get the nurturing you need when you need it.
- Enjoy it when other people treat you kindly but take the primary responsibility for seeing that good things happen for you.

And in the next few chapters, we're going to look at some ways that you can do that...

Chapter Thirteen
Build More Positive Energy

In the last two chapters, we talked about knowing what things support your positive energy and making taking care of yourself one of your priorities. Let's look at other ways that we can build and support our positive energy levels.

One of the simplest and most adaptable ways to build positive energy is gratitude work. The Law of Attraction tells us that we draw to us more of what we focus on, so focusing on what's positive and working in our lives creates better energy and a more positive reality than giving our energy away to what we don't like.

Want better energy? Start by looking around for what's good in your life. Count your blessings. When things go awry, see what's still working in your situation, deal with things and turn your attention back to what's positive as soon as you can.

Doing this helps to keep your energy at positive levels and keep you out of a downwards spiral.

Regular meditation can clear negative energy and build calm, focused positive energy. Whether it's breath work, a moving meditation, being present in the moment or a guided meditation, meditation does a body good.

We talked about meditation back in the chapter on clearing your mind. Some key points:

- Find types of meditation that work for you.
- Find types of meditation that work for your routine.

- Set up your space to make it easy to meditate. (Headphones for guided meditation, comfortable seating, clear space for moving meditation.)
- Playing peaceful music in the background as you do other things can induce a meditative state.
- Build a routine.
- Link meditation to parts of your present routine. (Breathing meditation to start the day, meditation snack…)
- Post reminders to meditate. (Screen saver, index card that says "breathe".)

Then make sure to do it, and keep doing it.

One useful variation of meditation is visualization, a process where you close your eyes and picture the changes that you want actually happening.

To do this:

- Find yourself a time when you're less likely to be disturbed.
- Turn off your phone.
- Sit or lie down comfortably. (If you think you might nod off, it's better to sit.)
- Have your arms and legs uncrossed (so they don't fall asleep and distract you.)
- Do a simple breathing relaxation, like we discussed in the chapter on clearing your mind;
- Then close your eyes and picture what you want to achieve.
- Make the visualization as vivid as possible.
- Include as many of the 5 senses as you can. What sounds do you hear? What do things feel like?

- Visualize as long as you like or as works for you;
- Be sure to build in a process where you return to your body before leaping up to do something else. Breathe deeply. Become aware of your body and the world around you.
- Open your eyes when you're back again.

Those are the basics. How you play with them is up to you. Different people have their different ways of visualizing things. There are three more visualizations in the appendix at the end of this book if you want to try this technique.

Repeat when you can. The more you put your focus on something, the more you increase your odds of attracting it into your life or manifesting it altogether

Make sure to picture yourself as part of your visualization. I heard about a man who wanted a red sportscar. He decided to visualize one to attract it. He visualized, but forgot to include himself in the picture.

A week later, the sports car turned up. His neighbor bought one.

Visualization is good for building your confidence and willingness to try things. It's been used to support building physical and mental skills (like sports ability) and, in a pinch, in place of actual practice. It can also be helpful in attracting or manifesting things, people or situations that are currently not in your life.

Your unconscious mind believes whatever you tell it. It will do it's best to create or attract whatever reality you show it, even if it currently isn't happening. Make your visualization as realistic as possible and you'll both raise your energy and increase the ability to attract your goals.

If you're looking to create changes in your life,

especially positive changes, visualization can be very helpful.

We all have beliefs, conscious and unconscious ones. Some of those beliefs are helpful to us, and some of them are not. Those beliefs tend to affect our lives, both by shaping the nature of reality around us and by affecting how we interact with that reality.

At that point, it's better to have beliefs that support us than that limit or sabotage us- but how do we release the dysfunctional ones and grab hold of ones that help us?

One way is by using affirmations.

Most of our beliefs are in our minds because we've been told them time and time again.

- You can't make money doing what you love.
- It's a dangerous world.
- It's not what you know, it's who you know.

And so on...

Some of them are things other people told us. Some of them are ones we've told ourselves. They're all in our minds, whether helpful or not, because of repetition;

And repetition is how we change them. Get rid of the unhelpful ones. Replace them with beliefs that serve us better.

Affirmations are brief statements that are said or written repeatedly to rewrite our beliefs in ways that are hopefully more helpful to us. An affirmation:

- Is positive ("I always have the money to pay my bills" as opposed to "I don't bounce checks".)
- Is easy to say.

- Does not use words like "no" or "not". (The unconscious mind doesn't hear them. If your affirmation says "I am not clumsy", your unconscious mind hears "I am clumsy" and you'll find yourself tripping more.)
- Is expressed as something that's happening now.

It's also helpful to start small. Begin with an affirmation that isn't true yet but that you can see as possible ("I have the money I need to pay my bills." as opposed to "I am fabulously wealthy beyond my wildest dreams.") Big goal affirmations can work too, but are more likely to trigger inner resistance. This can make it harder to shift your energy and achieve what you're trying to do. Smaller steps are less likely to trigger that resistance, which means they tend to activate more quickly and easily. Once that happens, you can take another step up; and as you see smaller goal affirmations work, it can build belief so that you're ready to take bigger steps.

Studies find that repeating an affirmation a thousand times installs it in your subconscious as a new belief, and ejects other less functional beliefs that conflict with it. Many people find they start to see results well before getting to a thousand.

You can say your affirmations or you can write them out. (The teacher who had you write things repeatedly on the blackboard actually had a good idea.) I tend to repeat my affirmations in groups of ten because it's easier for me to keep track of where I am.

Better beliefs can raise your energetic level and help you have a better life. When you need better beliefs, affirmations are one good way to develop them.

Got sticky beliefs that you want to release but don't seem to be able to let go of? Find yourself repeating self-destructive patterns? (Same drama with different people?) Do you sabotage your own success?

You may have unconscious beliefs that aren't working for you. These beliefs may be:

- Things that worked for you at one point but no longer do;
- Societal standards that don't really apply to your life;
- Erroneous "lessons" you've taken away from personal experiences;
- Things that people taught you in an attempt to protect you, but that limit you instead;
- Or other beliefs that are wrong for who you are and how you're living.

Many times, such beliefs can be rewritten with techniques such as affirmations, but some beliefs have deep roots. It can be hard to let them go, even if you want to.

At that point, E.F.T. is a good way to clear out unwanted beliefs. Emotional Freedom Technique (E.F.T.) is a system that combines affirmations with tapping on points on your energy meridians. It was originally designed to help people with phobias and P.T.S.D., but it also works well for releasing those stuck beliefs that are hard to let go of. It's quick and easy to learn and quick and easy to do, and it works like a charm.

We don't have the space in this book to explain all the facets of E.F.T., but you can find directions easily on the internet by searching "Emotional Freedom Technique".

Give it a try for the ideas that won't let go.

Another way to raise your energetic level is to do something creative. Creative activities:

- help us to focus on the process,
- give us some control over our world,
- give us a feeling of competence,
- and result in a tangible result which can make us happy.

Think of creative activities as being like another version of the meditation snack we did early in this book. It focuses attention on something we enjoy, screens out other stressors, and gives us positive feelings of competence, control and creativity.

So whether it's painting or cooking or ballroom dancing, find the way you like to exercise your creativity and make room for it in your life.

Joy is good for your energy. Creativity is too.

While we're talking about ways of building a positive energy field, it's worth noting that there are a lot of systems of energy work that can be used for this. Some of these are:

- Acupressure,
- Acupuncture,
- Reiki,
- Therapeutic touch,
- Run Valdyr,
- And a whole lot more.

We don't have space here to explain how you do all

of these systems, but you can find more information in books, New Age stores and online, amongst other places.

Some of these systems need significant training to do successfully. (Some even require a license.) Some you can learn to do yourself. Some you may want to hire someone else to do.

In any case, when you're talking building and maintaining positive energy, one good way is energy work.

Even with the best of intentions, we all have bad days- days when our moods get blacker and our energy rides along. One thing that can help us to stay on track is to get ourselves an energy buddy. Energy buddies help each other by:

- noticing when you're getting negative or going downhill,
- reminding you in loving ways of things you can do to feel better,
- sharing their own good energy, which may help to lead your energy upwards again,
- and doing other things to keep you mindful of your energy and support you in keeping it positive.

It's important to note that energy buddies have a two-way arrangement. When one of you starts to have problems, the other is there to support you and help you get back on track. By helping each other to be aware and supporting positive energy, everyone benefits.

Don't go it alone, especially if you're living in interesting times. Find your buddy, or two or more. Find your tribe and help each other to keep your energy healthy and positive.

In this life, we all need a little help. Pairing up with one or more energy buddies can help all of us to be aware of our energy and do what we can to keep it positive.

There's lots of different ways to build a positive energy field and keep it in a positive range. Not every way will be the right way for you, but fortunately there's so many options that you're pretty sure to find one or more methods that suit you.

The important thing is to find the methods that work for you and to commit to doing them on a regular basis. When the default setting on your energy is positive, you'll be healthier, happier, more resilient and better able to cope with whatever interesting times may bring to you.

Find the ones that work for you and start making them a part of your life.

The Energy Around You

Chapter Fourteen
Warding to Protect Your Space

Earlier in this book, you learned how to protect your personal energy field from outside energy by shielding. You've learned how shields work, how to create them and how to adjust them for your individual needs.

Having protected your personal energy, let's look at how to protect the energy of the spaces you spend time in using warding.

What's warding? It's a way to protect the energy of a location- to keep negative or unwanted energy out and good energy in. You can ward your room, your apartment, your home, your land. You can ward your cubicle or office at work. You can ward any space you have some control over against outside influences, making it easier to concentrate on what you want to do without being swamped by drive-by energy.

Sound good? Let's get started.

Warding a space is setting up protections to keep unwanted energy out. Unwanted energy can be negative, dysfunctional, or excessive energy. Before we start putting up wards, the first step is to clear and cleanse the energy already in the space, so we're not locking unwanted energy inside with us.

There are lots of different ways of clearing the energy of a space. One way to do this is with a mixture of salt and water. Combine these in a spray bottle and spritz it around the area you're trying to clear. You can also use a cloth moistened in saline solution to wipe down items, and the walls and floor in your area.

Another commonly used method is smudging with

sage, sweet grass or rosemary. Use a bundle of the herb you choose and place it in a fire proof container. Light and then extinguish it, so it puts out gentle smoke. Waft the smoke through the area you are trying to cleanse.

One variation of smudging is smudging with sound. The sound you use depends a lot on what sounds you like and what's appropriate to your situation. You can use a bell, or singing bowl, or drum. You can clap or stamp or sing. Move around the area you're clearing, making your sounds, with the intention that unwanted energy is cleared and stagnant energy set in motion. In places where the sound gets muffled or muddy, concentrate extra sound there to clear out blocked energy, until you hear the sound clear and become more normal.

You can close your eyes and visualize unwanted energy being blown away. You can also just set an intention that the unwanted energy is leaving now.

For any of these methods of clearing energy, make sure to move your clearing method throughout the space to make sure you get the whole area. Rotate in each room so that you face each direction in turn. (Counterclockwise is better because it's more efficient for breaking things up and getting rid of them.)

Combine any of these methods with a physical clearing or cleaning of the area.

Finally, be sure to combine your method of clearing with setting the intention that any energy that is negative or excessive or not helpful to you is expelled, and that only positive supportive energy remains.

After you clear the energy, the next step is to cast a circle. Casting a circle is a process of creating a protected space by using your intention. There's lots of different ways of casting a circle. Many people personalize them using guardians or symbols from their own spiritual paths, such as angels, totemic spirits or personal guardians. Give some thought to what symbols might be personally helpful for your wards.

Here's one basic method of casting a circle.

Start by marking the points of the compass, which are called the cardinal points. If you're casting a temporary circle for things such as spiritual practices, you'd use candles. If you're casting a permanent circle to ward an area, you use crystals instead of candles. These act as "repeaters", keeping the circle up even if a person or physical object crosses it.

- Start at the crystal in the East. Say "Spirits of the East, Powers of Air, guard this circle and all within it."
- Move clockwise to the crystal in the south. Say "Spirits of the South, Powers of Fire, guard this circle and all within it."
- Move clockwise to the crystal in the west. Say "Spirits of the West, Powers of Water, guard this circle and all within it."
- Move clockwise to the crystal in the north. Say "Spirits of the North, Powers of Earth, guard this circle and all within it."
- Move back to the crystal in the east. Say "The circle is cast."

Include the intention that the wards not only protect from unwanted energy on all four sides, but also above and below you. As you ward your space, set an intention that all negative, unwanted or excessive energy will be kept out of the space by your wards, and that positive, helpful and healthy energy will flow freely.

Once you've cast your circle, you need "repeaters" to make it last long term. Crystals make good repeaters. The best ones for the job seem to be double terminated quartz crystals.

Place your repeaters at the cardinal points (north, south, east and west) of the area you are trying to protect.

If you are inside, you can mount them in containers or stands, such as the wooden candle cups that you can find in craft stores. If you are protecting an area that's outside, you can bury them.

In addition to clear quartz, you may want to augment your wards with other stones.

- Black Tourmaline.
- Smokey Quartz.
- Blue Kyanite.
- Jet & Amber together.

Jet and amber convert negative energy to positive. The other stones act to ground out negative energy.

Once you've set up your first set of wards, you may want to expand the number of circles around your space. Having more than one ward gives you layers of insulation against random outside energy, and provides levels of protection which can be helpful, depending on the situation.

One example would be one set of wards inside your bedroom, another inside of your home, a third on the outside and a forth surrounding the property your home sits on. This would make your bedroom a calmer, quieter haven from an energetic standpoint. That can be particularly helpful for sleeping or when you're sick. It would also give some basic energetic shielding whenever you're on your land with protection increasing as you go into the house.

There may be times when you need to take your wards down.

- If you're moving and the warded space will no longer be your space.
- If there are confrontations or stressful events inside of the warded space, and you need to do a major clearing of unwanted energy.
- If you want to add to or change the intentions, you have used while warding the space.

If you need to take your circle down, this is one way of doing it:

- Start at the crystal in the north. Say" Spirit of North, Power of Earth, go if you must, stay if you will."
- Turn counter-clockwise and face the crystal in the west. Say "Spirit of West, Power of Water, go if you must, stay if you will. "
- Turn counter-clockwise and face the crystal in the south. Say "Spirit of South, Power of Fire, go if you must, stay if you will."
- Turn counter-clockwise and face the crystal in the east. Say "Spirit of East, Power of Air, go if you must, stay if you will."
- Say "the circle is open".

If you have taken your wards down to reset them, do any energy clearing or cleansing you need to do as soon as possible and then put the wards up again as soon as you can. If you are leaving the space permanently, taking them down is good enough.

We've talked about warding spaces that belong to you, where you have sufficient privacy and control to do a formal clearing and warding, but what about other spaces, the ones you share with other people?

It's possible to ward places like your office or cubicle at work, your parking space in a communal lot or garage, or your room in a hotel. Indeed, depending on the excitement/ craziness/ competitiveness of these spaces, warding them may be a really good idea to help you keep centered and able to do what you need to do.

The procedures for doing this, however, are slightly different. To ward common areas, you may need to be discrete, in order to avoid exciting comment or disturbing others.

For clearing, smudging with smoke is inappropriate to no- smoking settings, but smudging with sound can usually be done without bothering people. Dependent on your setting, humming, singing, clapping or stomping can be used to clear unwanted or stuck energy and move it out. You can also use salt and water as part of cleaning your area, setting an intention that it will also clear unwanted energy; or just use visualization or setting an intention by itself.

For warding, you can use tiny crystals as repeaters and position them so that they're not obvious. Follow the procedure for casting a circle from earlier in this chapter, but run through it in your head, as opposed to out loud.

In a more formal shared setting, such as a work

space, you may want to come in a little early or stay a little late, so that you can concentrate on what you're doing without being distracted.

You may find that, after you've done this, people comment on how calm and relaxing your work space is. Smile, thank them politely, and enjoy the energy.

One other quick note; if you've warded, and the energy of your home feels better for a while and then starts to feel a little funky, it may be good to check your repeaters. Sometimes they get displaced.

Awhile back, this happened to me. I thought I was just imagining things at first. When the feeling persisted, we checked and found that one of the repeaters had been knocked out of alignment during driveway modifications. Once we returned it to where it belonged, everything felt great again.

If you've warded and things start to feel more prickly, it may be illness or stress in your life, but it also may be that your wards need to be realigned. It's worth checking.

You've protected your personal energy field and you've warded the spaces that you spend the most time in. You've cleared yourself of unwanted energies and thoughts and beliefs that don't serve you. You've figured out who and what build your energy and who and what drains it. You're working on having more of the first and less of the second

Now it's time to take the spaces you warded and adapt them so they support building and maintaining positive energy. More on that in the next chapter.

Chapter Fifteen
Crystals and Energy

In the last chapter (warding) we talked about using crystals as repeaters for keeping wards up and running long term. There are other things we can do with crystals to support positive energy and clear negative.

Crystals are types of stones with energy fields. Different kinds of crystals have different types of energy. All crystals are better for some tasks or situations, and not as good for others. Everybody is going to have their own personal favorites.

Crystals can be used as tools, as noted in the wards chapter. They can be worn or carried to add their energy to the energy field of the person wearing them. They can be placed in an area to affect the energy of that space. There's lots of different ways to use crystals, and we're going to get into some of them in this chapter.

Let's look at crystals that can help us build positive energy, and the ones that don't.

Before looking at specific crystals, let's talk a little about how to cleanse them. Many crystals have picked up outside energy. The energy they're holding is not always the kind of energy you want around you. It may be negative and drag your energy into unwanted ranges. It may be excessive, and make you twitchy or jumpy. It may be perfectly fine energy but someone else's energy and you want your crystal's energy to be interacting with you.

The way you deal with that unwanted energy is to clean the crystal, just like you clean an apartment before you move in or your car after a long road trip. You clear out unwanted energy so the only thing left is the energy of the crystal itself. (That energy is why you brought it into your life in the first place.)

There are quite a number of ways to cleanse a crystal. Some ways include:

- Holding it under running water while setting an intention for unwanted energy to be carried away. (Please note that certain crystals are water soluble and this method should not be used for them. When in doubt, check online or in a good crystal reference book.)
- Leaving it exposed to sunlight and /or moonlight for a specific time. (I like a month unless there's some kind of time crunch.)
- Letting it sit covered by a solution of salt and water. (Some crystals are water soluble and can be eaten away, so watch which crystals you use this method with.)
- Bury it in the earth, or at the roots of a plant.
- Visualize it being cleansed of all unwanted energy;
- Or a combination of the above.

There are more methods besides that but that gives you some options to start with.

Some crystals are self-cleansing but many are not. If you don't cleanse them, they'll build up energy which can change the effect they have on you and your space.

When do you cleanse them? I'd start with always cleansing any stone you bring home, whether it's self-cleansing or not. (As my grandmother used to say "You don't know where it's been…") Once you've got your crystals all squeaky clean energetically, clean them when you feel like you need to. A lot may depend on things like:

- How much stress or negative energy you've been dealing with,
- What your life is like in general,
- The other people and things in your space and how they affect you,
- The nature of the world around you,
- And other things that affect your energy.

The crystals may be taking up some of the energetic slack for you, but they can only do that if you maintain their energy. How often is right depends on what feels right for you and your life, so, just as you monitor your own energy, it's a good thing to check-in with your crystals every now and again to see if they need cleansing.

And now, on to specific crystals.

When it comes to general, flexible, all-purpose energy, it's hard to find a better choice than clear quartz crystals. Clear quartz is like a little energetic battery. Its basic energy is neutral, but it can be charged with energy for a specific purpose, such as healing or protection. It can be used in tools, such as the repeaters mentioned in the warding chapter earlier in this book.

It also has a tendency to pick up energy from the world around it, so it should be cleansed on a regular basis.

Rose quartz is a form of crystal quartz, and is pink. It has very gentle, soothing and loving energy, and can help with stress and anxiety, as well as healing the emotions. It's a good friend in challenging times.

Rose quartz should also be cleansed regularly.

Hematite is a crystal that absorbs negative energy. It can be useful for grounding and stabilizing you. It's worth noting that, when it absorbs too much energy, it has been known to shatter.

And then there's stones that cleanse themselves. Certain crystals will take unwanted energy and ground it out into the earth. They clear their own energy, leaving you free to spend your time on other things.

Some good examples of self-cleansing stones that ground out negative energy are smoky quartz, black tourmaline and kyanite in all colors (but especially black kyanite.)

Amber and jet take things one step further. In combination, amber and jet not only absorb negative or unwanted energy, but also transform it into positive energy. That's a great combination, especially in interesting times or when you are dealing with crisis.

Jet can be hard to obtain these days, but if you can find some, pairing it with amber can be a useful technique to keep your energy positive.

Before we finish, let's talk about crystals you might want to avoid during interesting times.

For instance, amethyst. Everybody loves amethyst and it's a beautiful, useful stone, but one of its gifts is that it makes you energetically and psychically more sensitive. Great if you're trying to develop your metaphysical gifts; but if the energy around you is stressful or overwhelming and you're already having problems dealing with it, amethyst will not necessarily be helpful. At that point, you might want to put it away for a while until things calm down a bit.

Amethyst is also a stone that needs to be cleansed.

Opals have been known to increase emotions, whether positive or otherwise. If you're stressed, these might not be the crystals you want to carry.

While you're at it, you might also want to avoid some of the higher energy stones like moldavite, azeztulite and Tibetan tektite. Stones like these have a lot of energy, and if you're already having problems dealing with excess, unwanted or negative energy in your environment or situation, you don't need to add to the energy you have to juggle. Save stones like these for calmer times, when you have the breathing space to get to know them and work with them.

Please remember, these are not bad crystals (there are no bad crystals), but some crystals can make you more open to the energy around you or increase the amount of energy you have to manage. If you're already overwhelmed by the energy around you, this may not be the effect you're looking for. More is not always better.

Crystals are useful energetic tools and can be an important part of your plan or keeping your energy positive when you're living in interesting times. Think about what crystals might be a good match for you and your life, and then see if you can bring them into your world.

Chapter Sixteen
Your Space and Positive Energy

Why is it important to build more positive energy for ourselves, and to boost our personal vibrations to as high a level as possible? Well:

- Positive energy supports our health in body, mind and spirit,
- It boosts our personal resilience, which helps us to recover from challenges more quickly,
- It helps us to see things more clearly which helps us to make better decisions,
- It gives us the energy to take action, when action is appropriate,
- It helps us attract more positive people things and experiences into our lives,
- The more time we spend with positive energy, the more it becomes our habit or set point, and the easier it is to get back to it when we are knocked off center.

These are some good reasons to build more positive energy. These are some of the reasons to make building positive energy an ongoing part of our lives, as opposed to a once in a while activity.

Let's look at how to make your surroundings support your positive energy.

In past chapters, we talked about ways that you can be ready to nurture yourself. To have surroundings that help you do this, you can:

- Know what people, things and activities tend to

build your energy, as opposed to draining it.
- Have a list of these things and keep it in one or more places where it's visible or easy to access when you're feeling drained. (When you're down, you sometimes forget what you can do to lift yourself up again.)
- Know the supplies you need to increase your energy- music, books, movies, comfort foods, creative supplies and so forth. (Everybody has different supplies.)
- Keep those supplies in stock and easily accessible to use on an ongoing basis.
- Set your environment up so it's easy to do the things that build your energy. If that's dancing, have space clear to dance and a music system set up. If you paint, have a designated painting space with your supplies ready to use.
- Build a positive and healing environment that supports your energy. Use colors you like, comfy furniture, tools that work well, textures that feel good. Sometimes little factors make the biggest difference.
- Surround yourself with things that inspire you.

If looking at your space puts a smile on your face, you're doing it right.

Want to make it easier to build good vibrations? Let's get more specific about setting up your environment so that it's easy to nurture yourself and so you can start doing it at a moment's notice.

- Have books that inspire or comfort you shelved in a specific part of your book shelf, where they're easy to find.
- Have recordings that make you want to dance or bring you peace stored near your sound system, (with headphones ready to go, if you like them.)
- Have lotion or hand cream with a scent that makes you smile on your sink or bedside table, so it's easy to give yourself a quick treat.
- Is your chair comfortable? How about your desk or counter? Having furniture that fits you and feels comfortable can put you in a far better head space.
- Look at the little items you use every day. Do they work easily? Do they work well? Are they broken? Are they difficult to use? Are they a color that pleases you or do they feel good when you pick them up? Sometimes pretty stamps, a stapler that works well or an already sharpened pencil will bring more ease and grace into your life than an expensive tech toy.
- Some people like new items that are fun or make them feel pampered. Some people like old things that connect to family or a bygone era. What's important is having the kinds of things that support your positive energy.

Look at your home, your office and the other places you frequently find yourself in. Are there ways that you can tweak them so that you're happier and your energy is higher? Think about the little adjustments that can make a big difference to you.

Music and sound can be a good way to support health, happiness and positive energy. It's good to know what kinds of music or background sounds (such as white noise or sounds of nature) make you feel better and which ones drain you.

You may find that you need different types of sounds for different tasks.

- Hard rock for dancing and building energy.
- Sounds of nature to calm down and de-stress.
- White noise to focus.

Be aware of the different kinds of sound and how they affect you as an individual, so that you can make a conscious choice about what kinds of sound to have in your environment.

One kind of sound that might support your energy is silence. Some folks need quiet background sound to calm down, and others need an absence of sound altogether. Knowing which suits you for different tasks can help you make better choices.

Headphones can be a help. Sometimes you're sharing space with someone whose needs are different from yours at a particular moment. Sometimes you need to shut out a particular sound. Sometimes you need to focus, such as during a guided meditation, and headphones can help with that.

Finally, just as many sounds can build positive energy, some feed negative energy. Be aware of the sounds around you, and if there are some that are draining you or splitting your focus, see if there's something you can do to resolve that. Put on headphones, either noise cancelling or playing white noise. Adjust the load in the dryer that's thumping. Turn off lights that hum if you're not using them. Turn down (or off) the sound effects on your computer or the radio in the other room.

And, if you can't deal with negative sound in any other way, contemplate a change of venue for the moment. Maybe there are street repairs going on and you might want to go to a coffee shop for a while. Maybe this is the hour when your neighbor practices playing the bagpipes. Rather than drag your energy down, sometimes it's time to be elsewhere for a bit.

The bottom line is that sound can soothe you and build your energy or it can drain you. It's helpful to know which sounds meet your individual needs for different tasks, and it's also important to remember to use that knowledge to build your energy.

Make sound you enjoy a part of your environment. You'll make it easier to have positive energy.

It's good to have your space support building positive energy, but keep in mind that, when you're living in interesting times, there'll probably be times when you'll need a little more. Life happens, and not always in a positive way. It's good to have techniques and supplies accessible and ready to go on those occasions when life is especially challenging. Some options are:

- Comfort foods.
- Soothing music or environmental sounds recordings.
- Movies that help you regain your strength or your center.
- Comfortable clothing.
- Remedies for physical symptoms (ice pack for head ache, pain relief gels, homeopathic stress remedies.)
- Books that comfort or inspire you.
- Movies that help you to "cry it out" so you can go on.

- Someone to call who listens well, will make soothing noises or will bring you soup.

Extra challenging rain will fall in everyone's life. Before it storms in your life, think about the things, people and activities that help comfort you, find your center again and regain the strength to carry on. Make a plan and have the supplies ready to make it happen when you need to.

Have a plan to make healing easier.

It's important to take responsibility for keeping your own energy positive.

- Shielding and warding help keep negative energy out.
- Grounding helps clear us of negative energy.
- Knowing what raises our energy and drains us lets us know what will help us take care of our energy.
- Making nurturing ourselves one priority means that we stay positive and don't crash and burn.
- Building surroundings that make it easier to raise our energy means that we're more likely to do it.

And people are one of the most important part of the things around us when it comes to building and keeping good energy.

You've gotta find your tribe, and that comes next…

Chapter Seventeen
Find Your Tribe

Earlier in this book, we talked about getting yourself an energy buddy so you can help each other by keeping an eye on your mutual energy levels. An energy buddy is a good idea, but there are lots of other ways that people affect our energy levels.

- Some are needy and can drain your energy.
- Some are supportive and can build your energy up.
- Some are jealous and can intentionally try to trash your energy.
- Some contribute to the positive energy of anyone around them.

The people around you can have a massive impact on your energetic levels, positive or negative. Let's take a look at how we can make that work for us.

The first step is finding your tribe- people who feed your energy as opposed to drain it. These are the people you'll want to spend more time with because you'll help keep each other's vibrations positive.

They say your tribe is made up of people on the same mission as you are. I don't know if I totally agree with that. I think your tribe can be made up of people with an assortment of paths, missions and beliefs, as long as you all treat each other with respect. Indeed, I believe that sometimes a group that's not homogenous but is respectful can be a very good thing, as it opens you up to viewpoints and ideas that you might otherwise never run into.

We've talked about how to tell the difference

between people that build your energy and those that drain it. You listen to your body and see what it has to tell you. It's also good to think about what things are important and what are not. The buddy who tells bad jokes may have other habits that offset that, whereas the person who's always in crisis and in need of rescuing may be more maintenance than you can handle.

Give it some thought. Are the people you spend the most time with making you stronger or tearing you down?

Go find your tribe.

How do you find your tribe? There's lots of ways to do that, but let me give you some ideas to start with. Begin by thinking about what you're looking for in a friend.

- Kindness?
- Intelligence?
- Humor?
- Honor?
- Support?

It's not a one size fits all universe, so it's good to know what you're looking for.

One important aspect that I think most friendships should include is give and take. Your friendship doesn't have to be 50/50 but you should both have positive contributions you're bringing to the table, and balance is important. You also don't have to contribute the same things. Maybe your friend is lousy at giving advice, but is always there for you when times are tough. Keep in mind that the actual people may not be a perfect match for what you have in mind, but your idea can help you when you look for people with these characteristics.

Next, take your picture of the kind of friend you're looking for and think about where that kind of person might hang out.

- Special interest groups?
- Bookstores?
- Sports venues?
- Churches?
- Classes?

That gives you an idea of where to go yourself to make contacts and start finding your tribe.

Finally, it's good to have an idea of who you're looking for, but remember to also leave yourself open to serendipity. Some of the best, truest friends I've ever had didn't look like the kind of people I wanted in my tribe at first. Leave room for the unexpected gem who may turn out to be exactly who you're looking for (even if you don't know it yet)

Once you've found your tribe, it's important to have reasons to spend time with them. Not just for energetic feedback- don't just save them for when you're in crisis. Spend time with them, as much good time as possible, because the energy of those good times builds the energy of your relationships and sustains you all when times get tough.

Find or create reasons to get together for positive experiences and fun. Go places together. Talk on the phone or online. Eat together. Work on projects together. Share things or experiences you know your tribe would like. Fun builds trust and good energy, and trust and good energy make more positive energy for the group.

Having people who like you and support your dreams is good for your energy. It nurtures you and builds a feedback loop as you nurture others in return. Hanging with people with positive energy is also good for your energy via something called entrainment.

In a vibrational situation, entrainment is a process where all of the vibrations gradually move into harmony with the strongest prevailing vibration. It's like the way that the strongest voice in a singing group can pull all of the other voices offkey or keep them on key.

A group of people will tend to have an energetic setting it defaults to. When the overall vibration is positive, it'll tend to pull everyone upwards. If one of you drops into a negative range, the group energy will help to pull him upwards again without conscious effort on anyone's part.

Don't be needy, but do invest some time, energy and effort into your relationships and your tribe. The strong ties you are building will support better energy for you all.

As you spend more time together, you'll get to know each other better. One of the things that includes is understanding how each member of your tribe communicates. That's important because there may be times when one of you needs to tell another that he's stressing or crashing. Even if we're aware, we don't always notice that in time for ourselves and having someone else to cue us in can make it easier to recover more quickly.

Some people like to be told these things gently. Some folks prefer a straightforward "in your face" approach. Some people's communication styles vary, depending on where they're at. Knowing the best way to communicate with your buddy can help because it lets you give them important information without either sounding critical or like you're pussyfooting around.

Part of being friends and supporting each other is knowing the best way to tell your buddy when he needs to pay attention and maybe do something without causing further trauma. It's one of the benefits of hanging with a positive group of people who know each other well.

Some people are good for our heads and our hearts and our energy. Some people are not. It's amazing the number of times that the "nots" suck up most of our time and energy and attention.

Everybody has times when they need a little help from their friends, but some people are just chronically needy. They're constantly in crisis, whether the crises come from external sources or whether they create them for themselves.

Some people get their sense of power and strength and wellbeing by sucking the life out of people around them or by controlling them. For some people, the only way they can be on top of things is to put you down and dance on top of you.

Whether its needy or controlling, the energy is relationships like these tends to be flowing mostly in one direction- away from you. There's not a lot of give and take- there's mostly give.

At that point, you need to step back and take a look at things. You need to figure out what you can give. You have to figure out what you want to give. You need to figure out how much you can give without burning yourself out and how you can maintain your own energetic levels.

Part of this may involve improving your ability to nurture yourself or finding other ways to build up your own energy; and part of this may involve figuring out how much you can give and where's your priority for giving.

If you learn lifesaving, they teach you that, when you approach someone who is drowning, the first step is to approach cautiously and not let that person pull you both under. That applies in this case as well.

So, pay attention to where your energy is going. Notice who builds your energy and who drains it. Decide how much of your energy you want to give away and how much you feel you can give without crashing and burning yourself.

And use that awareness to make choices so you can maintain your own energy as well as help others.

Sometimes you'll have people in your life that are not good for you, but that you can't walk away from. Annoying in laws. Nasty bosses. Unpleasant co-workers.

If they're bad for your energy but you can't invite them out of your life, you should probably be thinking about how to set some boundaries.

- Learn how to say no. A lot of us have problems with this, but the truth is that there are a lot of things that we don't have to do just because somebody else wants us to.
- Limit or control the amount of time or energy you give them.
- Be prepared to say that certain behaviors are bad for you. If you want to explain why, feel free, but remember that you're not obligated to justify this. You can just say "I'm not willing to do that," or "I only have this much time to spend on this."
- If they're being abusive, feel free to walk away for the moment. If they're haranguing you on the phone,

you can say "I can't talk like this. Call me back when we can talk without yelling" and hang up. If you're at a gathering and they're harassing you, you can say "I have to go," and do it. Interrupting inappropriate behavior is one way to possibly change it.

If you think you might be in a situation where you'll need to set boundaries, plan it out in advance. Be prepared that the other person may try to change the conversation. Bring it back on topic and if they won't co-operate, do what you can to end it for the moment.
Last, if you have a tough situation where you need to set boundaries, make sure that you do something to bring your energy back upwards afterwards. Nurture yourself. Hang with your tribe, or do whatever speaks to you.

The people around you have a definite effect on your vibrational level and can bring you up or drag you down. It's good to be aware of who does which in your life, and give more of your time, your attention, your love and your resources to the folks that are good for your soul.
Find your tribe, be sure that you spend time with them, and watch your vibration climb upwards

Chapter Eighteen
Taking Control

We've become more aware of our energy fields. We've made ourselves a safe energetic space, grounded out our negative energy and gotten in touch with what energizes us and what drains us. We've taken a good hard look at the things, people and experiences in our lives and how they affect us. We've made nurturing ourselves one of our priorities and taken steps to fill our lives with more energy and less drain. We've turned inwards, building a strong nurturing relationship with ourselves to give ourselves the energizing input we need. We've looked outwards, to find the people who can help us support more positive energy.

And now, having learned ways to work with our own energy, let's look at how our interactions with the world around us can build more positive energy.

One of the better things you can do for yourself when living in interesting times is to do what you can to move out of the victim state of mind.

When you face challenges, they can seem insurmountable, like we have no choice other than be at the mercy of what the world sends our way. There may be some truth in feeling vulnerable, but the bottom line is that we usually do better if we start believing that we can make a difference, instead of being helpless victims.

Even when situations seem overwhelming, there's usually some way, large or small, that we can start to regain some control of our worlds. Looking for that point of control and taking action once we find it can help break us out of a cycle of helplessness and start our energies moving upwards again.

One way is to know that we can choose our focus, and that focus makes a difference energetically. Put more energy into what's wrong in our lives, and we'll tend to draw more of that and other things like it to us. Put our focus on what's positive, and we'll tend to attract or create more positive things, people and experiences.

The belief that there's nothing we can do keeps us from seeing things we can do. The idea that there are things we can do helps us find solutions that were invisible to us.

Look around you. Start by looking for what's working. Somedays it may be really basic things, like you have people who care about you, you have the ability to choose your focus or even just that you're breathing, but there's almost always someplace you can start.

Acknowledge what's working and be grateful for it. Count your blessings. Pray. Use other kinds of gratitude work to bring those positive things into your view, appreciate them and keep them in your focus.

Build habits that support focusing on what's working. Count your blessings while you brush your teeth. At the end of your day, list what went right. When something positive happens, quietly thank the universe.

When you find yourself focusing on what's not working, stop and think. It's important to acknowledge all parts of your life, especially those that you to deal with them. You don't want to give a majority of your energy to them though. Focus enough to do what needs doing
and then return your focus to something positive.

Just remember to keep most of your focus on what is working in your life and how you can create more of that kind of thing.

When taking more control of your life and how you interact with the world, one trick is to ask yourself the right questions.

What makes a question the right question? It's a question that gives you more hope, more faith, or more control of your situation. It's a question that helps you find possibilities or solutions, not get bogged down in the problem. It's a question that helps you move forwards, as opposed to just feel trapped.

Some examples?

- "How can I solve this problem?"
- "Who do I know who could help?"
- "Where can I get more information about this?"
- "What can I do to feel better about this situation?"

Don't ask yourself "Can I fix this situation?" Ask "How can I fix this situation?" Some situations can't be totally fixed, but starting with the premise that there is an answer and you just have to find it is more likely to help you find answers than acting like there is no solution at all.

Ask yourself questions that empower you and work from the concept that there is a solution. If you do this, you're more likely to solve your problem and you'll have better energy to solve it with.

When parts of our lives feel out of control, there is power, strength and meaning in taking what control we can. Making an active choice to take control of our lives, in small issues or big ones, gives us a feeling of strength and competence, breaks us out of negative thinking and brings our energy levels upwards. It helps to:

- Find and do things that are meaningful to you.
- Do things where you can see a tangible result.
- If you can't tackle big tasks, start with small ones. The energy you get from completing a small task can increase your energy so you can handle a larger one.
- If you can't get control of a situation that is draining your energy, find another area where you can gain or regain some control. Taking control of some area in your life, no matter how small, can increase your vibrational level so you can go after the bigger issues.
- Follow through and complete commitments you have made, whether to others or to yourself. Keeping your word and completing tasks can give you more energy and a feeling of competence and relief.

Taking control can build your vibrational level and help you to dig your way up out of any energetic pit you have ended up in.

Taking control doesn't mean that you have to have total control. It's not a perfect universe, and the idea that you can make it that way isn't very realistic.

One big cause of victim mentality and the negative energy that goes with it is perfectionism, the idea that anything less than perfect is no good at all. Many people are afraid to do things because they're afraid that they'll be harshly judged by others. Many people beat themselves up if they can't do something perfectly the first time, and end up never trying anything at all.

Truth be told, imperfection is part of learning and the human experience. If a baby tried to walk, fell once and thought "Nope. Never trying that again…", we'd be a world of people sitting around on our bottoms and never going anywhere.

At that point, one of the best things we can do is to let good enough be good enough. If we can't completely fix a situation, do what we can to make it as good as it can be. If you've tried your best, that's all you can do. Enjoy what's working, as opposed to focusing on what's not working yet. Use the energy that generates to give you strength to accomplish other things.

It's important to remember that taking control doesn't mean that you have total control of everything in your life. There's so many people and factors in the world that the idea of total control isn't realistic. Holding onto that idea can make you very unhappy. Do what you can and let good enough be good enough.

Taking control of our lives is one way to build positive energy. It's important to remember that sometimes it's better to take control and sometimes it's better to let go, though.

As I've said before, what you focus on is what you tend to draw more of into your life, whether positive or negative. This can work for you or against you.

Keeping your focus mostly on what's not working in your life tends to drop your energy levels lower and attract more dysfunction into your life. While some problems need some focus to fix them so they don't get worse, there's an awful lot of things that don't really need your energy. Giving them too much of your energy can take away the time, energy and focus that you could use to
have a happier, healthier, more successful life.

It's important to know this. Sometimes you're putting energy into making a problem situation better, but sometimes you're just pouring your energy into a ravenous black hole that will suck you dry, never be satisfied and always want more.

There comes a point at which you need to stop and think "Is the energy I'm giving to this situation, activity, experience, or person helping or draining me?" and "Is it realistic to think things will get better, or is the energy flow permanently one way?"

At some point, you may decide that you need to cut down on what you give this person or issue, or even let it go altogether. Spend less time on the news and more on stories that inspire you. Spend less time with people who tear you down and more with people who've got your back. Let go of that job that kills your spirit and find a better way to make a living.

Sometimes, the best thing you can do is let it go, and find new, more positive things to give your energy to. The only way to do that is to pay attention to where your energy goes and how that makes you feel.

Taking control of our focus builds positive energy which help us to attract more experiences, people and things we want into our lives. Taking control in the world around us builds a reality that supports our positive energy and helps to raise it even higher.

When you're faced with interesting times, the first step is to take stock of your personal energy and to do what you can to bring it back to a place of positive resilience. Once you've done that, look at doing what you can to gain more control over your own experience and corner of the world, and you'll find that it gets easier to keep your energy at a higher level

And that feels great

Positive Energy For Life

Chapter Nineteen
Check Where You're At

We know how it feels when our vibrations are low. We know how to check for it and we've identified at least some of the things that cause it. We know how it feels when our vibrations are higher. We know how to check for it, and we've identified at least some of the things that cause that as well.

What's the next step? Making sure that we're staying in touch with our energy fields- that we're checking our condition on a regular basis.

There are lots of things that we know are good for us to do but we don't always do them regularly. Eating right. Getting enough sleep. Exercising.

Add checking your energy level to the list. Even when we know what's happening, many of us don't check our energy until we're reeling because we're so depleted. That's the point where it's hard to get back to a good place.

Let's think about checking in with our energy levels.

One of the reasons we need to check our energy on an ongoing basis is that life happens and things change. That can mean changes in our energy levels, some short term and some for the long haul.

When you find there are negative changes in your energy levels, you should do what you can to clear unwanted energy and shift your energy upwards as much as you can. There will be times when you may need to shift your expectations of what your standard energy is like, but it's still good to do what you can to keep your energy as high as it can be in order to attract better experiences, be as healthy as possible and have the best life that you can.

Your body is talking to you.

We talked about this earlier in this book. Your body tries to tell you when your energy is high or low, when you're being drained, when your energy is being fed, when you're in balance and when you're not. It has lots of useful information for you that help you stay healthy, happy and positive in body, mind and spirit. All you have to do is to listen to it.

That's the problem. Many of us don't listen. Many of us try to "tough it out". Many of us ignore drain until it hits crisis levels. Many of us are so busy multitasking or thinking three steps ahead that we lose track of what is going on in the present moment.

That's a problem. We do need to learn from the past and look to the future, but we also need to remember to be present in the present. We need to be here now, not only so we can learn and benefit from and enjoy whatever's going on right now, but also so that we don't go out of center and end up spinning into a crisis. A crisis tends to eat more time than we save by multitasking or looking three steps ahead.

In meditation, they speak of being here now. That's good advice, especially if you use it to check-in with your body and your energy so you can do what you need to do to keep yourself centered, grounded and in balance.

Be here now, and listen to your body,

Do it on an ongoing basis.

We know what we need to do. We want to do it. We want to listen to our energy and keep it in good shape. We want to do it on a regular basis.

But things happen and we forget.

It takes a while to build a habit or a routine, and until

you get it down, it's all too easy to lose track and end up not doing what we know we want and need to do.

Until we get that habit down, it's good to build in reminders and supports, to keep us on track and doing what we need to do.

- Hang reminders on your walls in places you often look.
- Put a reminder on your dashboard.
- Put one on your screen saver on your computer.
- Put them on your phone.
- Set an alarm to remind you to breathe or relax or check-in with your body on an ongoing basis.
- Tie checks in to activities that are already habits. (Brushing your teeth? Driving to work? Going to bed?)
- Ask your energy buddy to give you regular feedback because you're trying to build a healthy habit of positive energy.

While you're building a pattern of checking your energy on a regular basis, build cues into the world around you to remind you to stick with it for your own benefit and the benefit of the world around you.

The final step to checking your energy is to remember to do something about that energy. If it feels low, stop and do something to feed your energy and build it back up. If it feels good, stop for a moment and enjoy that good feeling.

If you looked at the gas register in your car and it was riding close to empty, you'd stop at a gas station and fill up again. If you didn't, you'd run out of gas and end up sitting by the side of the road, waiting for a rescue.

Your body is like that. It's important to check your energy regularly, but it's not enough just to check. You need to check your energy regularly and then do what you need to in order to put your energy at the right levels and keep it that way. That's an essential step for having a happy, healthy life, and making your way through both interesting and calmer times.

It's good to check-in with your energy, but it's easy to forget to do so. That's when we get off center and let our energy drop into the negative levels.

Studies find that it takes at least 30 days of doing a process before we make it into a habit. Checking in with your energy is a habit worth having, so it's good to do what you can to make it easy and automatic.

Look at things you can do to support checking in regularly so that you keep your energy at a healthy, happy level. Let your environment support you. Gather folks who will remind you.

And listen your body.

Chapter Twenty
Rinse, Repeat, Build a Routine

We've now been through basic energetic strategies for dealing with challenges and living in interesting times. We've learned about:

- energy and our own energy fields,
- how the world around us affects our energy fields,
- how our energy fields can affect the world around us,
- how to protect our energy from unwanted outside influences,
- how to get rid of negative or unwanted energy, whether it's from outside influences or a do it yourself project,
- how to know what feeds our energy and what drains us, and that we need to have more of the first in our lives than the second,
- that we need to listen to our bodies to know when we need to maintain that energy or boost it back into positive levels,
- how to build positive energy,
- how to protect our spaces and how to create spaces that support positive energy,
- that some people will support positive energy better than others,
- and that we need to take care of our energy on an ongoing basis.

Whew. That's a lot of things- and now we're to the final step. We need to build habits that support positive energy, both now and as an ongoing process.

We need to rinse, repeat and build a routine…

The first step in building your routine is becoming more aware. As I've said a number of times in this book, you need to listen to your body. If you listen, it has plenty to tell you about when things are going well and when you need to do something to get your energy back on track.

Know the signals your body sends you when things are going well and when they're not. Do you feel relaxed? Energized? Excessively twitchy? Like you want to cry for no particular reason? These are all messages about the state your energy is in.

To listen to your body effectively, you need a routine. If you're checking in with yourself randomly, it's too easy to get distracted by other things and not notice your energy's going off the rails until you crash and burn. For that reason, I'd recommend tying check-ins to things you already have in your life. These can be:

- Established routines (ex: Check-in while you brush your teeth.)
- Schedule points (Check-in when you wake up and when you go to sleep.)
- Regular breaks (Check-in at each meal or snack.)
- Times of day (Check-in at 10 and 2.)
- Or any other way to make check-ins a habit.

Find a way to make check-ins a regular part of your everyday life. Check-in more than once a day. Build a routine for multiple check-ins, so if you miss one, you have others to take up the slack.

Studies say that it takes 30 days of daily action to build a new habit. The trick is remembering until that habit is formed. When you start building a routine, you may need reminders to work your practice until it becomes a habit. Try things like:

- Writing it on your calendar,
- Making an appointment with yourself to meditate or check-in,
- Sticking Post-it notes with "Breathe" or "Check-in" in places around the house that you're likely to look at frequently,
- Add a Post-it reminder to your car dashboard,
- Set a timer on your watch, phone or computer to remind you,
- Get a positivity buddy to remind you to work your energy when you may forget to.

There's lots of ways to remind yourself to check your energy and take action to keep it positive. Choose the methods that you like best to make your routine work for you.

You want to have a routine for checking in with your body, but you also want to make yourself aware of impromptu signs that something is off. Look for things like:

- Ongoing exhaustion.
- A series of colds, stomach upsets or other low-grade ailments.
- Feeling irritable or weepy out of nowhere.
- A pattern of tripping more, banging into things more, more small injuries.
- Reacting to situations in a more extreme way than you normally would.

- Busywork or distractions.
- Putting things off.
- The desire to leave an area or run away.
- Traveling but finding reasons to delay getting where you're going.

All of these are things that can happen as a normal part of a normal day, but all of these and things like them can also be symptoms of something messing with your energy. Pay attention, and when things like this come up, stop and ask yourself:

- "Where is this coming from?"
- "Does this seem like my usual reaction, or is it over the top?"
- "Is this my problem, or is someone else's energy affecting mine?"

How you deal with this situation depends a lot on whether it's an ordinary bad day, or whether something is interfering with your positive energy. The remedy can depend on the cause, so pay attention and figure out whether you've been caught in the path of some drive by negativity or whether it's something that time and chocolate will resolve.

You've been checking in with your body and listening to what it has to tell you? Good stuff! But that doesn't complete your energy routine. You need to check-in regularly, and if your body tells you that you're off center or off track, you need to do something about it.

Let's say that again. If your body tells you that you're off center or off track, you need to do something about it.

You need to do something about it. You need to do something as promptly as possible. And you need to keep checking in until you find your energy returning to a positive level or as positive as possible.

Knowing that your energy's going downhill doesn't do you much good if you don't take action. Think about it for a minute- if the light indicating your brakes had failed went on in your car, you wouldn't just look up and say "Oh, hey, I've got no brakes…" You'd pull over, call a tow truck, get those brakes looked at, do whatever you needed to do to keep yourself and others safe until the situation could be resolved.

This is kinda the same thing. If your energy is going down, you need to do something to bring things back to normal and keep yourself and others safe.

For this reason, it's good to leave wiggle room in your schedule to ground or shield or nurture yourself as needed. Know your priorities so you know what you can put off to make room for energy maintenance. These can be based on what needs to be done sooner, what's more important, what feeds your positive energy as opposed to drains it or other criteria you've chosen. Make nurturing yourself one of those priorities. You don't want to pack your schedule so full that you don't have room to take care of yourself. (Indeed, that's often one thing that'll move your energy lower in the first place. That's two good reasons to leave room for flexibility and rest.) The important thing is to set your priorities by what is most helpful to let you have a happy, healthy, meaningful life.

Once you know your priorities, it's good to do them first. Do what you can with the time, energy and resources you have, and when you run out, that's all you can do.

Listen to your body, know when it's telling you that

things are off kilter and then take action as soon as you can to put your energy right again. The time, energy and stress you'll save by doing it right away more than compensate for what you put into it.

If your energy's going lower, you need to do something to bring it back up again. What should you be doing? For starters, check to see whether outside energy is affecting your energy, and do what you can to limit or eliminate that negative influence. This includes things like:

- Cutting down on the number of things you're trying to complete in one day,
- Finding ways to delegate tasks that drain you,
- Swopping tasks with people who don't mind them as much,
- Call screening,
- Limiting time with people who make you angry or tired,
- Avoiding or limiting activities you don't really enjoy,
- Doing holiday shopping early to beat the rush.

You can also check whether part of the problem is your own expectations. Sometimes we put so much pressure on ourselves that we turn a good experience into a misery. Sometimes we need to let good enough be good enough.

Sometimes we need to remember to let things go. There are some things we can't fix and continuing to try when we've got lots of evidence of this is like pouring energy into a bottomless pit. If you've done all you could, it may be time to let go and stop letting it drain you.

Once you've patched up the places where your energy's being drained, then it's time to build more positive energy. We've talked about some options earlier in this book, but it's important to remember that what works for you is probably different from what works for other people. You need your own reference library of energy building activities.

Try some of the activities listed earlier in this book. Try other things that you enjoy doing that aren't listed here. Listen to your body as you do them and afterwards. Is your body sending you signs of positive energy? Then maybe this is something that should become part of your regular routine. Make a note of it and move on to try something else.

It's good to use energy building activities as treatment when your energy is dropping, but it's also important to build a routine that includes them on a regular basis. Why run yourself into an energy crisis when you could avoid it by just taking care of yourself in the first place?

Take your list of energy boosting activities and look at how you can build them into your day or week or month. Could you do a conscious snack or a walking meditation every day? Could you have books that inspire you ready to read? Could you dance, or draw or tell bad jokes several times a week? Having a routine which includes ways to bring yourself back to center and raise your energy upwards on an ongoing basis will keep you healthier and
happier and give you a better life

Make a commitment to treat your energy well. Make an appointment with yourself. Write it in your datebook if you need to. Then push that energy in positive directions on an ongoing basis. You'll be glad that you did.

It's good to understand how your energy works. It's good to do things to move your energy into a more positive state. To get the most out of this book, it's important to not just do this one time. Life is a journey and keeping your energy positive and focused is an ongoing process that should happen throughout the rest of your life.

You need to build good energy habits and build a routine that incorporates those habits so that they become a normal part of your life. Ways of getting in touch and staying in touch with what your body has to tell you. Practices that clear negative energy and boost your energy back to the positive vibrational levels it belongs at. Methods to remind yourself to follow your practices and not let things go until you're in trouble again.

For this you need a routine. Since this is not a one size fits all universe, there's no one routine that'll work perfectly for everyone. That's why this book is filled with different options of ways to do different things- so you've got a selection of options to choose from and can design a routine that best suits you.

Your routine doesn't have to be like anyone else's. It doesn't have to live up to anyone else's standards or ideas. What it does have to do is to fit your needs and your life, to make it easier to take care of your own energy without getting to the brink of crisis to do so.

You'll know when you've got the right routine. It may take a while to get used to it, but it'll feel good once you've got it down and you'll find that your life gets better. You'll be able to handle challenges better. You'll be better able to handle to cope with living in interesting times

Start thinking about what belongs in your routine. Try things out and see if they fit.

And then see how your practices fit together for the

long haul, and enjoy your routine.

Chapter Twenty One
Living in Interesting Times

In the end, we come back to the beginning, but with more knowledge about dealing with living in interesting times. We'll all have interesting times at points, whether health challenges, a family crisis, the loss of a job or social upheaval in the world we live in. It's part of the human condition, and having skills that help us survive and thrive during these times can make the difference in how we go through them and how we come out of them.

And these are the points we all need to remember:

- Positive energy supports health, happiness, resilience, and the ability to make better choices.
- Positive energy attracts more positive things into your life.
- If you take responsibility for your own energy, you have more control over your life.
- It's important to know what drains you and what builds you up.
- Once you know that, it's important to do more of the things that support your positive energy and less that drain you.
- It helps to create an environment that supports your positive energy.
- It helps to find other people that support positive energy and spend time with them.
- It helps to have a plan for what you'll do to build and support positive energy.
- And it helps to do that plan on a regular basis. Rinse and repeat.

No matter what happens, positive energy makes you better able to deal to whatever the world brings you, so find that things that work to support your positive energy and make them a regular part of your life.

I wish you the best, whether your times are interesting or not; and when times are interesting, I wish you the wisdom and energy to cope with them. Keep your head, keep your center, and come through those interesting times.

Appendix

A Light In The Forest

(This visualization is designed for clearing unwanted, excess, or negative energy.

This is a structured visualization, where most of the story is set up for you. You can read this and picture it in your head, or you can record it and listen to it while you visualize.)

Close your eyes and relax. Feel relaxation sinking into every part of your body. Every muscle, every bone, every nerve, is heavy, so heavy, and very, very relaxed. Be aware of your breath as you breathe in and breathe out, breathe in and breathe out, and with every breath, you are more and more relaxed.

Picture yourself in a green, green forest. The trees around you are tall and strong and green and tower overhead. Here and there, a ray of sunshine beams down into the deep green shade of the forest. The air is crisp and clean and smells wonderful as you breathe in and out, in and out. It's quiet and still except for the little sounds of a living wood, sounds of birds and little animals and green things growing. You are moving through these woods and you feel wonderful and safe in this beautiful place.

You come to a clearing now, and, in this clearing, is a woodland pool, nestled in the heart of the wood. Coming closer, you see this pool is full of light, a beautiful fluid light that contains all of all the colors you can imagine. It glistens and shines, rippling and gurgling like water but shining with light.

You dip one finger into the light. It feels wonderful; warm enough to be healing and comforting, and cool enough to refresh you as well. It feels so good that you decide to take a dip.

You wade in and as the light covers each part of your body, your body feels more healthy and relaxed. Your feet feel great and your legs, your hips and your stomach and your back. Your hands and arms dip into the light, and your chest and your shoulders and your neck. Your entire body is feeling healthy and relaxed in the light. Take some time and enjoy this healthy, relaxing, energizing feeling.

As you move to the far end of the pool, you see a cascade of light splashing into the pool, renewing and refreshing it. You move into it. The light falls on all sides of you, in the front and the back and on the left and the right. It even passes through you, washing away any illness or energy that is negative or unhealthy or that gets in the way of your happiness. That unwanted energy is washed away. Your body fills with positive healing light.

When you're ready, when you feel the time is right, when you feel completely cleansed and healed, you move out from under the light fall, feeling healthy and positive and energized. Everything that limited you is gone, washed away by the light. You feel wonderful as you come back out of the pool.

It's time to come back now. At your own speed, become aware of the room, aware of your body, aware of your breathing, and, when you are ready, slowly open your eyes.

The Book of Answers

(This is a visualization for getting answers to questions you're having problems answering in other ways. Start by deciding on your question.

This is a partially open visualization. Part of the story is set up for you. There are spaces left for you to fill in, either in advance or with your unconscious mind as you go along. You can read this and just picture it in your head, or you can record it and listen to it while you visualize.)

Close your eyes and relax. Breathe deeply and feel the relaxation sink into every part of you.

Picture yourself sitting in a comfortable chair in a place that feels comfortable and safe. In your hands is a large and impressive looking book. The title on the cover is ***the Book of Answers.*** When you open the book, you find that the first few pages are blank, except for the word ***ASK*** at the top of the page.

There is a pen secured by a loop to the outer edge of the cover. Taking the pen, you carefully write your question or the issue you're wondering about on the open page- and before your eyes, an answer slowly appears on the page in front of you. You may see:

- Words,
- Still pictures,
- Moving pictures,
- More than one piece of information,
- Or any other combination that will give you useful information.

What answer did you see?

If the answer isn't clear to you, you can write another question to give you more information.

Take all the time you need to absorb the information you receive and figure out what it means to you.

And then, when you're ready, slowly open your eyes and come back to the physical world.

This is an open visualization, where we set up a story that will help you to get in touch with your intuition and let your own inner wisdom fill in the answers. Your unconscious mind knows more things than your conscious mind does. A story like this gives it a way to get in touch with you.

Feel free to adapt this into something that works best for you. I chose a magical book, but you could also look into an electronic tablet, an enchanted mirror, a big screen tv or a mystical smart-phone and get the same effect if that's better for you. Choose the image that suits you best and use it to help you get messages from your intuition.

Make this into what works best for you or create other stories that help you to know and do things. The point is to tell a story that supports you and gives you more information.

Time Travel

(This is a visualization for finding long term solutions to challenging situations. If you're living in interesting times and you can't see how you're going to get through a situation, try this.)

It's a partially open visualization. Part of the story is set up for you, and there are spaces left for your inner wisdom or your unconscious mind to give you answers. You can read this and picture it in your head, or you can record it and listen to it while you visualize.)

Close your eyes and relax. Breathe deeply and feel relaxation sink into every part of you.

Picture yourself sitting in a comfortable chair in a place that feels calm and safe. You have a challenging situation. You need more information to resolve it in a way that's easy and positive for you. You're about to get this information by traveling through time.

Look ahead of you. You see many roads stretching out in front of you as you sit in your chair. These roads are paths into many possible futures that lie ahead of you.

Set an intention that you want to resolve your situation in a way that's easy, positive, healthy and what you want. Set an intention that you want to see the path that leads you there. Watch the other paths fade away. See a single path shine ahead of you.

Take a deep breath. Feel your body get lighter. Take another deep breath and then a third and feel your body float gently up out of your chair like a balloon.

Float gently forwards over the path that leads to the solution that you want. Floating is easy and feels great. As you float along over your path into the future, look down and notice the steps you take to get to where you want to go.

At the end of your path into time, you'll find another chair waiting for you. Gently and easily, drift down into your new chair and settle yourself into your ideal future. Look around you at this future. Get familiar with what it's like and what that means to you.

Next to your chair is a small table, with a pair of binoculars on it. These are time binoculars and will let you more closely examine the steps you took along the way to get to the future you wanted. Pick up those binoculars and look back at the path that led you from now to the future, taking note of all you need to know to achieve your goal. Take as long as you like.

When you feel you're familiar with your ideal future and the steps you took to get there, set the binoculars down again. Take a deep breath, a second, and a third, and drift back over your time line from the future back to now. Settle back into your original chair.

And now, become more aware of your breathing; and your body. Gradually become aware of the room around you; and, when you're ready, open your eyes.

Once you've returned to the present, take a moment to review all that you've learned in your trip through time. (You may want to write it down.) This visualization can help you get in touch with your inner wisdom. It can give you insight that helps you to make better choices and move more successfully through interesting times.

Glossary

Affirmations - Brief statements said or written repeatedly to change your beliefs.

Aura- A layered energy field that surrounds us.

Cardinal Points- The points of the compass.

Casting a Circle- Creating a protected space using your intention.

Chakras- energy vortexes on many parts of your body.

Clearing – Removing unwanted energy from person, place or thing.

Crystals- Stones possessing energy fields.

E.F.T. (Emotional Freedom Technique)- Combines affirmations with tapping on points of the energy meridians to release fears, phobias or beliefs.

Empath- A psychic sensitive to emotions.

Energy Buddy- A partner who helps to monitor and maintain healthy energy levels.

Energy Work- Techniques for using energy to make things happen.

Entrainment- Process where one vibration comes into alignment or harmony with a stronger one.

Gratitude work- Noticing and giving thanks for positive things in your life.

Grounding – 1) Strengthening your connection with the physical world.

2) Using your connection with the Earth to release unwanted energy.

Law of Attraction- When energy is at a certain level, it tends to attract other people, things and experiences that also vibrate at that level.

Magick – energetic or non- physical methods of changing reality around you.

Meditation- Ways to clear and calm our minds, regain our centers, focus and break out of the cycle of negativity.

Monkey Mind- distracting or "chattering" thoughts.

Presence- Focusing on what you're doing at the moment and screening out other things.

Repeaters- Tools for keeping wards up long term.

Self-cleansing- Items that clear themselves of unwanted energy.

Self- nurturing- Giving yourself the attention and care you need to be healthy, happy and function at your best.

Setting an Intention- During energy work, setting a goal for what you want the energy to do.

Setting Boundaries- Taking control of how much time, energy or other resources you give to others.

Shielding- Technique for protecting your personal energy Field.

Smudging- Clearing the energy of an area with techniques such as smoke or sound.

The Gap- Space between stimulus and response, where meaning is attached to what's happened.

Visualization- Meditation where you close your eyes and picture changes you want.

Warding- Protecting the energy of a space.

Index

Advanced energy techniques 91

Amber and jet- 108

Amethyst- 108-109

Affirmations- 88-90

Aura- 15

Azeztulite - 109

Breathing meditation- 37-38, 86

Cardinal points- 99-100

Casting a circle- 98-99, 102

Cause- Effect – 43-44

Chakras – 31-32

Cleansing crystals- 105-107

Clear quartz-100, 107

Clearing –3, 22, 25, 29-30, 32, 33, 35, 51, 85-86, 97-98, 101-102, 151,

Clearing energy of a space- 97-98

Crystals-15, 98-99, 100, 102, 105-109

Emotional Freedom Technique- 90

Empath-15-16, 19-21

Energy buddy-92, 117, 135

Entrainment- 120

Free Will-3, 7, 29

Gratitude work-85, 126

Grounding- 25-30, 32-33, 108, 116,

Heaven and Earth meditation – 30-33

Hematite- 108

Kyanite -100, 108

Law of Attraction- 6, 85

Magick - 11, 25, 29

Meditation- 30, 35-42, 85-86, 91, 114, 134, 143

Meditation snack- 39, 40, 86, 91

Moldavite, - 109

Monkey Mind- 36-37, 39-40

Opals- 109

Presence- 39

Repeaters- 99-100, 102-103, 105, 107

Rose quartz- 107

Self cleansing- 108

Self- nurturing- 79-83

Setting an Intention- 17, 102, 106,

Setting boundaries- 67

Shielding- 15, 21, 33, 51, 97, 101, 116

Signs of positive energy- 145

Signs of stress- 65

Smoky quartz - 108

Smudging- 97-98, 102,

Smudging with sound- 98, 102

Stress- 1, 30, 35-36, 40, 51-53, 57-61, 64-65, 68, 73, 79, 91, 101, 103, 107-109, 114, 116, 120, 142

The Gap- 43-46

Tibetan tektite.- 109

Tourmaline, black- 108

Visualization- 17, 87, 153- 158

Repeaters- 99, 100, 102-103, 105, 107

Warding - 97-103, 105, 107, 116,

If You've Enjoyed This Book

While I hope your life has fewer "interesting times" and more peace and prosperity, I hope that, if or when those times come, I hope that there's information here that helps you weather the tides.

(I also hope that you've enjoyed the read.)
If this's the case, I'd invite you to

- Check out my other books at
  http://www.lulu.com/spotlight/CKane ,

  https://www.amazon.com/Catherine-Kane/e/B00BKPLSZK/ or

  https://www.barnesandnoble.com/s/%22Catherine%20Kane%22?Ntk=P_key_Contributor_List&Ns=P_Sales_Rank&Ntx=mode+matchall

- Visit my writing blog at
  https://catherinekanewrites.wordpress.com/
- Visit my Facebook page at
  https://www.facebook.com/Catherine-Kane-Writes-134304556668759/
- Write me a review on Amazon, Barnes and Noble, Good Reads or other places.
- Drop me a comment to let me know what other topics you'd like to see me write about.
- And if you have friends that you think might enjoy or benefit from my books, please share the word.

Thanks. I look forwards to seeing you again.

Catherine Kane

Who is Catherine Kane?

Catherine Kane is a writer, professional psychic, bard, Reiki master, story teller, Christian mystic, teacher, speaker, enthusiastic student of the Universe, maker of very bad puns and overachiever (amongst other things…) She is fascinated with things metaphysical, spiritual, self improvement and alternative health.

She has published six other books for the public so far – "Adventures in Palmistry", "The Practical Empath-Surviving and Thriving as a Psychic Empath", "Manifesting Something Better", "The Psychic Power of Your Dreams", "Magick For Pennies: Affordable Metaphysics For Everyone", and "The Lands That Lie Between" (an urban fantasy novel.) The odds are good that she'll continue to carry on in this fashion.

Visit Catherine at
www.CatherineKaneWrites.wordpress.com
and as Catherine Kane Writes on Facebook

Catherine can also be found with her husband Starwolf as Foresight at
www.ForesightYourPsychic.com,
www.ForesightYourCTPsychic.wordpress.com
or as Foresight on Facebook.

168

Also by Catherine Kane

Adventures in Palmistry

Your Destiny is in your hands – and you can have a hand in your destiny! Reading palms can empower and enlighten you, giving you the information you need for the adventure of life, and enabling you to help others around you. And it can be a lot of fun, as well. "Adventures in Palmistry" makes palmistry easy and fun. It will put the power of palmistry in your hands.

Magick For Pennies: Affordable Metaphysics For Everyone

Do Magick Without Breaking the Bank. Welcome to metaphysics, where intention, energy work and magick let us shape the nature of the world around us. It can be amazing, useful and fun, but sometimes can become expensive. Always something new to buy, and many things are not cheap. Magick For Pennies shows you how to fill your world with magick without emptying your wallet in the process. You will • Learn metaphysics basics and how magick works. • Explore metaphysics to find your magick. • Try an assortment of different types of energywork. • Know what's a bargain, and how to find one. • Learn about making your own magickal tools. • Make connections for your own unique journey. Your affordable magick is waiting for you. Find it with this book

The Practical Empath- Surviving and Thriving as a Psychic Empath

Do other people say you're too sensitive? Do other people's emotions overwhelm you? Do you carry abdominal weight you can't seem to lose?

You may be a psychic empath, tuned into emotional energy which can empower or drain you. To use that gift to help yourself and others, you need to learn skills that put you in control of your gift.

This is the book to help you do just that...

Manifesting Something Better- Easy, Quick and Fun Ways To Manifest the Life Of Your Dreams

We are always manifesting- so why don't we manifest something better? The world is made of energy and our own energy determines the things, people and experiences in our lives. Better energy-better life. The trick is to know how to use your energy to manifest the life you want. This book is here to tell you how to do just that. It's full of simple methods for improving your energy and working with it to manifest the things you want in your life. Easy, fun and practical. Are you manifesting something better? This book will give you the skills you need.

The Psychic Power of Your Dreams: Practical Skills for Working With Your Dreams For Insight, Information, Creativity and a Better Life

Your dreams are the doorway to your psychic self. We are all psychic- and dreams are the way most of us first get in touch with our intuition. Dreams bypass blocks and judgment, and put us in contact with our natural inner wisdom. It's easy- and this book will teach you how. You'll learn: • The types of dreams, (Which one are you having?) • How to remember your dreams, • A simple way to interpret your personal dreams, • How to dream to access your psychic ability, • How to deal with problem dreams, • And much, much more. Awaken your own psychic gifts through your dreams. This book will show you how.

The Lands That Lie Between-
An Urban Fantasy with Morgan and Sam

The day that Morgan lost her job, she knew that change was coming. She broke her lease, threw everything she valued in life, including her cat Sam, in her van, kissed her adoptive family goodbye, and started a cross country trek.

She knew change was coming. She expected that.

What she wasn't expecting was elves, or magick walking in the world around her, or the beauty and the danger of the Lands that Lie Between…

For more information on these books, please visit Foresight Publications at www.ForesightYourPsychic.com

www.ingramcontent.com/pod-product-compliance
Lightning Source LLC
Chambersburg PA
CBHW032042090426
42744CB00004B/98